SIN·SEER
LEADERSHIP

SIN·SEER
LEADERSHIP

A LIGHT-HEARTED

GUIDE TO MORALITY

IN THE BUSINESS WORLD

RAJ D. MOHAN

Published by Advantage, Charleston, South Carolina.
Member of Advantage Media Group.

ADVANTAGE is a registered trademark and the Advantage colophon is a trademark of Advantage Media Group, Inc.

Printed in the United States of America.

ISBN: 978-159932-378-7
LCCN: 2014950318

Book design by George Stevens.

This publication is designed to provide accurate and authoritative information in regard to the subject matter covered. It is sold with the understanding that the publisher is not engaged in rendering legal, accounting, or other professional services. If legal advice or other expert assistance is required, the services of a competent professional person should be sought.

Advantage Media Group is proud to be a part of the Tree Neutral® program. Tree Neutral offsets the number of trees consumed in the production and printing of this book by taking proactive steps such as planting trees in direct proportion to the number of trees used to print books. To learn more about Tree Neutral, please visit **www.treeneutral.com**. To learn more about Advantage's commitment to being a responsible steward of the environment, please visit **www.advantagefamily.com/green**

Advantage Media Group is a publisher of business, self-improvement, and professional development books and online learning. We help entrepreneurs, business leaders, and professionals share their Stories, Passion, and Knowledge to help others Learn & Grow. Do you have a manuscript or book idea that you would like us to consider for publishing? Please visit **advantagefamily.com** or call **1.866.775.1696.**

This book is dedicated to my dearest friend, God, and the Wisdom keepers who shine white light and want to show how everything still turns to gold, and my dear Mom, Dad, beautiful family and friends — you all know who you are and I'm lucky to experience in this lifetime how truly special you all are. I am forever in your debt in this sweet cycle of time.

With gratitude to Linda:

"To my sister, Linda,

Against all odds, you humbly agreed to take this journey through time with me, and tirelessly continued to enlighten my path allowing me to find my way forward - for that I am eternally grateful"

Tribute to Anthony Strano (1951-2014)

A life inspiring champion who soared above the limitations and imitations of materialism, ego and falsehood; giving us all insight on how to dispel the terrifying dragons of illusion, doubt, fear and worry.

To your golden soul, dear Brother, your physical presence will be deeply missed, but you will forever remain in our hearts.

Tribute to Robin Williams (1951-2014)

Thank you, Robin Williams for bringing light and lightness to the world with your inimitable wit and humour. You lightness will always linger making all our lives sweeter.

TABLE OF CONTENTS

Introduction | 11

CHAPTER ONE: A BEDTIME STORY | 19

The Golden Age Dreamscape

Iam on the Battlefield, the CEO as Soldier

The Intention

CHAPTER TWO: BACKGROUND | 41

Who Is Raj?

The Yoga of Humanity—The Path to Peace

Jackie Chan and Spiritual Growth

CHAPTER THREE: IAM'S ENLIGHTENMENT | 61

*AL, Alpha, the Almighty being,
Now Communicates with Iam*

Putting the Om Back into Commerce

The Titanic Life

AL's Soliloquy on Iam's Enlightenment

Virtue over Vice

Building Constructed by Vice

The Doorways of Hell

CHAPTER FOUR: BEING TRUE TO ONESELF | 87

Princess Diana, Prince Charles, and Infidelity in the Public Eye

Children of Hate

CHAPTER FIVE: BEWARE OF FALSITY | 101

Machiavellian Marketing

The Sickness Industry

John DeLorean and False Dreams

No Regrets

CHAPTER SIX: THE DEEPER IMPACT OF OUR CHOICES | 121

The Dogs of War

Heaven Can Wait

The Womb Can Be a Prison

The Frankenpharmacy

Snakes in a Capsule

CHAPTER SEVEN: ENLIGHTENMENT | 147

An Encounter

Sin-Seer Leadership

CHAPTER EIGHT: DECIPHERING THE MEANING AND MAGIC OF WORDS | 177

Wordz

Songz—My Pathways to the Soul through Rock and Roll

Essential Tracks

CHAPTER NINE: POLISHING THE JEWEL THAT IS YOU | 203

Your Eight Superpowers

END FABLE: ANECDOTE OF THE MONK | 217

SIN-SEER LEADERSHIP——SOURCES | 223

I n order to live and excel with honour, it is vital to understand the fundamentals of the blueprint and heartbeat of the soul, the conscience; one's true inner driver. This involves understanding the mechanisms by which it enlightens and guides us to excel in life. Many individuals either knowingly, or unknowingly, suppress the voice of their conscience. When witnessing a wrongdoing or an immoral act, which diffuses a bolt of lightning to their conscience, they either cry within, or scream out, 'Oh, how could he (or she) do this?

The reason is simple: though the conscience can never die, it can be intoxicated, or put to sleep.

In the world today, generally people develop a comfort zone in allowing their conscience go into a deep slumber, so they can carry on doing whatever they're doing, even if it is negative for themselves and all concerned. Then, one fine day, their conscience is rudely awakened, and like a snarling wolf, it bites them within, creating havoc in their lives.

To highlight the function of the conscience further, there is the legendary story of the old Cherokee chief who enlightened his grandson about a battle that goes on inside all human minds.

He said, 'My son, the battle is between two wolves inside us all. One is Evil—it is anger, envy, jealousy, sorrow, regret, greed, arrogance, self-pity, guilt, resentment, inferiority, lies, false pride, superiority, and ego. The other is Good—it is joy, peace, love, hope, serenity, humility, kindness, benevolence, empathy, generosity, truth, compassion, and faith.' The grandson was intrigued, thought about it for a pensive minute, and then fervently asked his grandfather, 'Which wolf will win, grandfather?' The wise old Cherokee simply replied, 'The one you feed.'

What is the modus operandi for feeding the good & virtuous wolf, and starving the bad one?

In order to recharge the batteries of the soul, people have tried many paths, keeping the expectation that tomorrow will somehow be better.

The mental and karmic battleground of Good versus Evil is beset with pyrrhic victories, conquests gained at such an overwhelming cost that, in the final analysis, it is almost equivalent to a loss. Currently, the battery of the soul has become discharged such that humanity frequently experiences a state of black-out, unable to discern right from wrong.

Every human being in the world experiences yoga. Yoga simply means a meeting, a union, a fusion, or confluence. The easiest and fastest form of yoga is simply 'remembrance'.

The *Bhagavad Gita* describes the epic Mahabharata war that clashes Good against Evil. When the virtuous warrior Arjuna realises that the evil enemy comprises of family and friends, his judgement becomes clouded, weakening his courage to face the truth, and thus paralysing his actions to engage in battle. In his moment of extreme doubt and procrastination, God, through the instrument of Sri Krishna, teaches Arjuna the Yoga of Royalty; the knowledge of the imperishable soul, and its union with the perishable instrument of the physical body, heart, and mind to play its part on the drama stage of life. He was enlightened that he was merely an instrument whose duty was to perform sukarma (good actions), and never to be concerned about the fruits of those actions. The performance of righteous actions guaranteed the inheritance of an abundant life. This is possible when the spiritual intellect, the third eye, the divine eye of realization is open, allowing the conscience, the inner compass of truth, the heartbeat of the soul, to fully and freely express itself.

The body is a transient vessel. It's changing by the millisecond, even if we cannot detect it. Deepak Chopra once said that up to 600 million blood cells are born each second and dying each second within each one of us. Still, we are trapped in the illusion that we are permanent beings. The fact is that the essence of life is a process of constant change. Chopra has also enlightened us further with the metaphor of the butterfly to suggest worlds of possibility inherent in our consciousness that can facilitate our own transformation: 'The imaginal cells lie dormant inside a caterpillar's body, becoming activated within the chrysalis to allow a butterfly to ultimately emerge. Like seeds of pure potential encoded into the caterpillar's DNA, imaginal cells are the ingredients of metamorphosis.'

The universal law in the *Bhagavad Gita* states, 'Ever change is the rule of the universe.'

The physical body needs the fresh food and the right nutritional balance on a daily basis; likewise, the mind also needs the right seeds of thought to maintain constant freshness. Positive silence is like oxygen for the mind which helps to keep the heartbeat of the soul fit and healthy.

Indeed, yoga is a simple term, and yet encompasses a wide meaning, having absolute significance in all our lives.

Andrew Marvell, the English metaphysical poet of the 1600s, also spoke of the misunderstanding and struggle between the body and the soul in his poem "A Dialogue between the Soul and Body":

Soul: O, WHO shall from this dungeon raise,
A soul enslaved so many ways?
With bolts of bones, that fettered stands,
In feet, and manacled in hands;
Here blinded with an eye, and there
Deaf with the drumming of an ear;

Body: O, who shall me deliver whole,
From bonds of this tyrannical soul?

In order prevent such discordant yoga based on ignorance of the true self, just as we have knowledge of the body and the faculties of our sense organs, we must seek to have the same clarity about the composition of the soul and its various faculties.

The body experiences suffering when it is deficient in any of its key elements: earth, water, fire, air, and ether (space). For the breath of life, one needs all five elements. When the soul is deficient in any of its original core qualities (peace, love, truth, happiness, and bliss), we can experience suffering in the form of isolation, or a sense of suffocation. When we are weak, the original qualities (virtues) adopt their alter ego or negative form (vices).

Ego is the greatest ignorance.

When relationships are perforated by the fangs of ego, and poisoned with its venom they become disjointed and fragmented. As the poison spreads, it can result in a complete communication breakdown which becomes the basis for many types of diseases. The *dis-ease* of mental imbalance will always lead to physical imbalance, ultimately manifesting *dis-eases* such as high or low blood pressure, heart disease, diabetes, psychosomatic disturbances, and sleep disorders, amongst innumerable others.

Where there's ego, there cannot be any union of love.

'A love-filled relationship is the deepest desire of the human soul', according to the spiritualist Anthony Strano. We have also seen this in classical British literature. Love is a central theme in *Jane Eyre*, a clash between the conscience (the heartbeat of the soul) and passion (the physical heartbeat), and the earnest longing to be driven by the truth. The inner struggle to discern true feelings from false, to discern the real diamond from the counterfeit gem.

It is said that true love conquers all.

Today, some people cry out to a superior being, or for angels to bring a drop of true love into their lives. America is a nation where angels don't just sing at Christmas time, but they're a year-round presence. A 2011 *Associated Press*-GfK poll shows that 77 per cent of adults believe in angels.

Yet, who are these angels?

The angels that communicate, protect and guide you are comparable to a clear conscience speaking to you from within.

A vast majority of people today live in a state of extroversion, totally occupied with the outer world through their sense organs, almost completely disengaged from reflective introversion, thereby divorced from the original qualities of the soul.

In order to achieve true mastery of one's life, one has to be able to detach from the five sense organs, and in a state of self-reflection be able to access the original inner qualities of the soul.

Depending on our mindfulness of these qualities, and accordingly the choices we make, we are either 'zapped' with power, or 'sapped' of power, resulting in experiencing either a state of bliss, or alternatively one of mediocrity. In general, humanity currently chooses to live in a state of mediocrity. As a result, the original qualities of the soul are present in varying degrees, but lacking in their original brilliance.

We can truly 'Live' when driven by our virtues, and yet we become the opposite, 'Evil', when we are driven by our vices. To quote Soren Kierkegaard, 'Life can only be understood backwards; but it must be lived forwards.' In truth life is a cycle, "what goes around comes around".

A cornerstone of Christianity is the karmic law of 'As you sow, so you reap', and 'love thy neighbour as thyself'. In reality, we all live in 'glass houses', and it is in this way that we must aim to perceive the world, whether with our families or those in business with us.

We need to be clear about our ultimate destiny and pay heed to Steven Covey's leadership habit number two: 'begin with the end in mind', so we are able visualise the outcome of any of our actions, to ensure that we sow righteous seeds and thereby harvest the best fruits, leaving behind a legacy of greatness.

The acquisition of accurate knowledge is analogous to an anti-snake venom serum; In effect, accurate knowledge is the antidote that neutralizes ego.

"SAPIENTIA FONS VITAE"
(WISDOM IS THE FOUNTAIN OF LIFE).

The power of wisdom evolves from true understanding. True understanding comes when I have the quality of humility. The word 'understanding' has within it the words 'standing under', which conjures up the vision of bowing down with humility; thus having the humility to understand, and by doing so, we acquire the power of knowledge to dispel the darkness of ignorance and negativity. Constant humility will keep my mind always open to new learning. The Japanese call it Kaizen, and Anthony Robbins calls it C.A.N.I. - Constant and Never-ending Improvement. I have coined the abbreviation W.I.P.E.— Work In Progress Eternally. This entails living in a constant realm of humility and openness to new ideas and experiences.

AUTHOR'S NOTE:

This book is a glass house, of course. I am aware that my frankness may cause offense. Please believe me when I say that is not my intention. I have tried, in complete good faith, to create a text that will be helpful to all.

— *RDM*

CHAPTER I

A BEDTIME STORY

THE GOLDEN AGE DREAMSCAPE

We will begin with a story.

The bright light from the full moon reflected uninhibited through the curtainless window, throwing its radiance over the vast, unfurnished bedroom. The moon's glow was aided by the kerosene lantern in the corner of the room. Deep brown eyes peered out of the top of the bedspread covering the child's body. With great innocence, the child pleaded, 'Mommy, can you now tell me the story?'

The soothing voice began, 'Once upon a time, there lived a king who ruled a land called the Golden Kingdom. It was the most beautiful place on Earth. The palaces were built with bricks of gold. The king's crown was golden and the beaches had golden sand, and even the peacocks had one golden feather each. Everything was perfect.'

'Can we go and live there?' questioned the child innocently.

'One day, my child. One day', replied the mother and continued with the story. 'The king's son, Prince Sukh, studied while playing because, in this land, studying was like a game. The lessons were drawing, playing, music, dancing, songs, and poetry. It was never boring.'

'That school is fun. Can I go to it? I don't like my school. Everyone fights and punches.' The mother sighed and patted her son's head. Her son's insecurity and restless nights had led to this ritual of storytelling each night, with the hope of soothing him into peaceful, uninterrupted dreams.

Trying to keep the child's thoughts focused on the kingdom's goodness, the mother continued, 'Prince Sukh loved playing the golden flute. All his friends would gather around him in the beautiful garden surrounded with waterfalls and dance and sing and laugh together. There was no sorrow in this land, only happiness.'

The child's eyes were heavy now and the lids were drooping. His mother knew just a few more lines would be enough. 'The kingdom was magical. Everyone could fly a plane no matter what age they were, so one day Prince Sukh decided he wanted to go for a ride. He sat in the airplane, pressed a button, and flew far off into the sky, far, far away. Far into the night sky where millions of stars twinkled and shone through the darkness.' The mother kissed the child's sleeping face and walked out of the room. 'Love you, darling. God bless, sweet dreams', she whispered.

'Far, far away. Far, far away', reverberated in the subconscious mind of the child, transporting him into another realm of existence.

Sleep peels the layers away and it is in this realm that one gets in touch with one's true inner identity: that of being a point of light; imperishable and eternal. The light that never 'dies' but grows dim and degraded over a period of time (our current state of amnesia) until we are able to 'wake up' once again, and connect with our true original identity.

Iam, the child, was transported into the unknown and into the secrets of a golden world.

There we were, diving deep into the beautiful golden river and then coming up, spluttering and giggling, comparing the size of the dazzling gems we had swooped up. Deep down on the bed of the river were jewels of all shapes and sizes, a veritable treasure chest of brilliance, sparkling and dazzling. This is our favourite game. Prince Sukh and I would scoop up as many of the jewels as we could in one breath and then kick our legs as fast as we could to get to the surface. The one with the largest stone scored a point. Then the whole exercise would be repeated until one of us reached 10.

The secret of this game was the deeper one swam, the bigger the gems one got. As our heads bobbed up and down the river, the scenery around us was beyond any imaginable sensory expectation. A land of super sensuous joy: All around us were palaces decorated with many coloured lights, lights of gold, lights of diamonds. The sparkling of colours merged and caused all the buildings to appear illuminated. Once the sun's rays fell on the diamonds and gold, it appeared as if a thousand lights were burning. Every palace had diamonds of nine colours, which created light of an extraordinary intensity.

The breeze served as a natural fan around us. The leaves rustled and the branches swayed, all the while creating a different kind of music to the ears. For as long as I could remember, it had neither been too hot nor too cold. The weather was always like spring. In the palace gardens, there was always an abundance of spring flowers, rainbows of rich, vibrant colours of all types of flowers beyond one's imagination.

The five elements of nature (earth, water, fire, air, and ether) were truly in unison with one another and the people of this land. Fruits were plentiful here. Whatever taste was required could be fulfilled with natural fruits. There were separate fruits for eating and drinking. 'Come on, Prince Sukh. Let's get some mangos. All this swimming has made me hungry and thirsty.'

As we swam to the riverbank, we could hear the birds, an orchestra of bird song. It was this sweet music that woke us up each morning.

As we ran toward the mango trees, the sheer abundance and diversity of fragrant fruits kept our hearts brimming with contentment. The lamb and the lion sipping out of the small puddle near the trees made us feel nothing could be more perfect. This was the definition of pure ecstasy, happiness beyond the senses.

Beyond the laughter and merriment, not lost in the gentle pull of the winds, not using the eyes to see that which lightens and brightens, not using the ears to be hypnotized by the musical magnificence, and not using the mouth to taste the sweetness of the first fruit of the season, but rather listening to the sound of silence within, in tune with the spiritual.

Here, the study of life was contentment, a need to know and gently anticipate the movements of the mind, and also to feel the pull of destiny. Just like the water of the river needs the accurate force of the current, so its course is undaunted; we had the force of the spiritual current to course smoothly through life.

As I grew up, I was totally sure of my immortality. When I got married to my childhood sweetheart, it was in this immortality that we found freedom, freedom from physical death in knowing that physical death only begets a new birth. We were uninfluenced, unaffected, and we constantly experienced the true essence of our beings. Our relationship was one of sharing, not giving and not taking. Our day was divided beautifully and the result of this balance was our clear conscience. Our 24-hour day was mapped out. We had eight hours to work, eight hours to spend with family and friends, and eight hours of rest, which was further divided by four hours of deep sleep and four hours of self-care and reflection.

Our son Khushi (happiness) and daughter Shanti (peace) were procreated through pure love and brought us endless joy, the virtue so strongly rooted in our minds blossomed in our heart, uplifting our soul, and brought great significance to who we are and what we do. We were complete in every way one could imagine.

My son Khushi giggled and happily announced, 'Daddy, I won. My stone is bigger than yours.' Shanti cheered, rallying for her brother. My favourite childhood game of diving deep into the lake and picking out the largest gems was now an all-time favourite. I looked at the gem in Khushi's palm and at the smallest gem I had picked out. The sheer lustre and brilliance of these stones never failed to touch my soul. Then a thought came to my mind, 'Children, the rules of the game are now going to change. It's not about who picks the largest "stone" but it's about who picks the "stone" which will shine the brightest once it is exposed to the sun.' The children cheered, once again.

The children were happy to dive deep again to decide which stone they would have to pick. Those were the days when no trace of negativity existed. Competition, challenge, and cheating were unheard of. Our entire lives were about living lives of peace, harmony, and happiness, with no thought of performing any actions that would scar the soul. 'Daddy! Daddy!' the sweet, melodious voice of my son rang in my ears. 'I'm going to come back and pick different stones every day and keep them in my room and see which stone gives off the most sparkle. I can play this game on my own now.'

Little did anyone realize that these stones were actually treasures that symbolized our true original nature, totally embedded with the original qualities of the soul.

'But only in dreams can men be truly free.'

—ROBIN WILLIAMS, *DEAD POETS SOCIETY*

*'A dream is not that which you
see while sleeping; it is something
that does not let you sleep.'*

—A.P.J. ABDUL KALAM, *WINGS OF FIRE*

IAM ON THE BATTLEFIELD, THE CEO AS SOLDIER

Travelling many light-years ahead to current day, Iam is in the trenches of Afghanistan when a sniper bullet flies towards the centre of his forehead.

The soldier had just been thinking of U2, the band, ironically named after a 'high altitude spy plane', and the songs that had influenced him.

'Bullet the Blue Sky', where Bono had requested the 'Edge' to put 'El Salvador through your amplifier'; 'Still Haven't Found What I'm Looking For' and waiting for judgment day to arrive. Another, a song by DMX called 'X Gon' Give It to You' (clean version) with which he had a holistic, cathartic experience—paradoxically feeling a positive aggression physically, emotionally, mentally, and, finally, on his spiritual plane. As the song entered his spiritual plane, Iam was able to see clearly how to fight the demons within. He has a revelation, an epiphany, a deep experience about the true meaning of that song versus the illusions that attack his mind. Just as the bullet enters, the sounds above him mix with his thoughts, as the U2 flies overhead.

Iam softens as the bullet approaches his forehead and he recalls 'Stairway to Heaven' by Led Zeppelin. The song flows through the corridors of his brilliant mind, and he experiences the truth while scanning the words with his divine intellect, the third eye.

There's no escape, as the bullet enters his forehead, except for Iam to go deep within to that original pool of peace, purity, and love. Another name for the soul is Vimān. Vimān is the inner temple or citadel, and also flying palace as described in Sanskrit epics. The experience of the flying Vimān can be felt when listening to Queensryche's 'Silent Lucidity', Hawkwind's 'Silver Machine', and Tracy Chapman's 'Fast Car': 'Starting from zero—got nothing to lose'.

Like an ejector seat of a burning plane, Iam is able to go deep within, disengage himself from the body, enter his Vimān, and escape at lightening speed into the sound of silence. The body experiences an explosion of liberation as the bullet enters the skull and travels into the physical brain so that all of the organs disconnect; the ultimate peaceful 'detachment' from the world. The Big Sleep.

This happens in the physical realm, when the bullet enters and disengages Iam's body, cutting into his brain. Iam enters the realm of peace within his soul so that he never experiences an ounce of physical pain.

The soul cannot be cut, burnt, suffer any decay, or dry out. The forces of nature capable of destroying physical elements but their combined actions have no influence on the soul. It is permanent, and imperishable. The soul belongs to time immemorial.

The Vimān launches itself at the speed of vibration, faster than sound and even light. The Vimān reaches its pure home in the space of vibration and the motionless body falls down in slow motion. As the soul connects with the Supreme Being, the body slumps to the ground, sending up a cloud of dust. The sun begins to be eclipsed.

As Iam hits the ground, the sun is eclipsed. A realization strikes all those present that Iam's dead body lying on the ground is related to these events of nature. Iam's slumped body does not have a face of pain. He's smiling in peace. Because that is visible, it's almost like the end of the world. The militants who killed him are mesmerised, because the face resembles, for each one of them, their personal loved one. It's as if they killed one of their own, closest to them.

All the militants are struck with a lightning bolt of inner realization, immediately forget their differences, and are fearful of God switching off the lights on them. As they approach the body, they realize it is lying in the perfect pose of Shavasana—the Hatha yoga pose of the dead body. The mental equivalent is detachment from the world. At the end of a yoga session, people lie down in a dead body pose. It creates a sense of detachment, making one understand and experience the truth that, indeed, we are transient beings.

There's no sign of physical injury; just a perfect and pure body, the face of perfect peace. The bullet that entered the forehead resembles a perfectly positioned *tilak*, the small dot on the forehead for which Hindus are famed. The *tilak* is normally put on the forehead in recognition of the soul. In Hinduism, one is perceived as an eternal being just passing through as an actor in this life. It's similar to Elizabethan times, the era of Shakespeare, when the elite and cultured left a skull on their desks as they worked, to keep them humble and remind them that one day they would end up the same. In *Bleak House* Dickens observed that 'Death levels us all'—a clear recognition that we are beyond the physical.

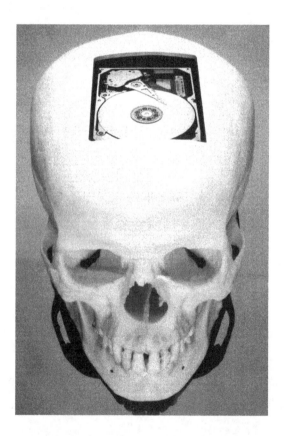

SOFTWARE OF THE SOUL CHANGES
THROUGH THE GOLDEN, SILVER, COPPER,
& IRON AGE IN THE CYCLE OF TIME.

The militants look at each other. Their differences dissolve as they experience a deep feeling of oneness. Simultaneously, everyone drops their weaponry as they shift their gaze upwards towards the accelerating eclipse.

The darkness is all encompassing, enlightening them. In oneness their bodies are no longer visible, only points of light. They come together, creating the shape of a Vimān. They speed off faster than the speed of light to the soul world, the world where the Supreme lives, to have an even deeper experience of their original oneness. The story now begins; Heaven Can Wait.

The Supreme Being, Shiva, reflects on the events of this *achanak* drama. *Achanak* means a 'sudden' turn of events. Which is the most powerful, the Supreme, karma, or drama? Only Shiva (God) can know completely about each and every secret of this sudden world drama and the current graveyard world of untimely death. But the world drama is all powerful, as even Shiva cannot influence and interfere with the current 'degraded' status of the world in this Iron Age. It is said, 'Nothing is beyond the power of prayer, except that which is outside the will of God.' What is it that is beyond the will of God? It is our individual karmic accounts upon which the Drama is driven. Every actor has complete free will to write his or her own script, and play his or her own part on this world drama stage accordingly. These personal scripts are the foundation of an individual's actions / karma, and the collective chemistry that evolves on the world stage is referred to as drama.

'As we walk through the valley of the shadow of death', is a true reflection of our current stage in the cycle of life, because there are no guarantees on our next minute. This is definitely the graveyard world of (*achanak*) sudden / untimely death. In today's age, 'anything is possible'. Hence, the current proliferation of 'possibility thinking' worldwide.

Unlike probability thinking which has an element of uncertainty, possibility thinking infuses one with a positive feeling about life. The famous preacher Robert Schuller explained that when one resorts to possibility thinking, driven by freewill and choice, the individual will tend to gauge the outcome in terms of 'what can be' enthused by hope, faith and positive anticipation; while one who is pre-occupied with a probability approach based on mathematical chance propelled by logic will compel him or herself to anticipate outcome as 'what may be'.

I've likened the word *birth* to berth, like a train. Your birth determines your berth, or the train of the life you take, and where that train takes you. Karma yoga involves sowing the seeds of action; the performance of one's actions, whether good, bad, or neutral, work on switching the train tracks of all of our individual and collective lives, determining our ultimate fate and destiny (destination). All that is required for success is a vision of the destination; the journey itself will reveal the means to take you there.

BIRTH DETERMINES YOUR BERTH, OR THE TRAIN OF THE LIFE YOU TAKE, AND WHERE THAT TRAIN TAKES YOU.

The Vimān can take any shape when the eight powers and all the virtues are mastered. It's like a rainbow, the colours of a prism, when all colours bleed into one. There's no single ego of one colour reflecting onto the world, but rather going into humble introspection and blending (cooperatively) with the other colours, powers, to finally reflect the supremacy of one colour, brilliant white, dazzling light, which dispels all the dark shadows of negativity.

Shiva reflects that the soldier with the dramatic departure from the body would normally be a *Bitkial Atma*, a 'wandering soul in the world of limbo', due to some unsettled karmic accounts. A soul that's stuck without a good future due to some traumatic set of events. Whenever there's a traumatic departure from the world, the soul enters into some realm through which it must suffer. Such suffering is a type of debt settlement in order to bring about a correction in its karmic accountability.

This is Iam. As the bullet enters, something in the supreme realm says, 'This soul is not supposed to suffer.' The bullet enters Iam, but he doesn't suffer. He is given birth again, once more, into a humble family, blessed with a divine intellect.

It is all to do with the cycle of life and death and rebirth. Rebirth— when a trauma teaches you another way of living—is the process of settling karmic debt.

There are many ways that life can teach you how to be reborn, another way of thinking, a paradigm shift, before death carries you away from this world. This is the aim of this book, and what it means for you as an entrepreneur, as a business person, seeking the moral ground in a chaotic world. You are Iam, a soldier and a CEO, about to be reborn into a new way of thinking about business: a moral one, based on ancient, timeless principles. This is the health over wealth, the immortal and imperishable component, versus the mortal and perishable. This paradigm is the foundation of everlasting sustenance, and of leaving a legacy of fortune.

THE INTENTION

One day I met a retired ex-soldier now living in Los Angeles. He used to travel to Iraq on business, and told me, 'You just won't believe what's going on currently in Iraq. The number of women drugging their husbands with sleeping pills so they can go out on the sly with their lover for the evening.'

I responded, 'That's life.' In this age of discontent, it seems impossible for a man and a woman to become as *one* in body, heart, mind, and spirit. Every relationship has something lacking, and so much miscommunication, consequently leading to an almost universal experience of discontentment. Everyone's thirsty for attempting to squeeze whatever sweetness they can find out of life. I heard of some couples who have officially separated due to irreconcilable differences, but who still sleep on the same bed, back to back, facing away from each other, because they simply cannot afford the cost of living separately. We also spoke at length about the plight of war-exhausted soldiers driven by psychotropic drugs, who return home to a life where nobody understands their traumatic experiences.

The plight of the soldiers is just a microcosm of the problems of the world at large. When your mind is prepared, you can dig deep within yourself in introspection, and then take the time to truly reflect on your outer world. Now, it's fine if you want to live a half-life, but this is targeted at everyone who wants to really find contentment in life. All of our actions have repercussions, and that's why I talked about the balance of physical health, mental health, spiritual, family and friends, and physical wealth. All of these elements are equally important. Basically, if you don't look after your body, you go to a hospital. If you don't look after your mind, you go to a mental hospital. If you don't look after your soul or spirit, life can become a living hell.

GEMS FROM THE OCEAN OF WISDOM

'Balance is the real foundation of a blissful life. Keep this in mind constantly, and your present and future will always be bright.'

The directives given and the experiences described in this book will, I hope, lead you to experience a more balanced life. There's a Showtime series in the United States, 'Shameless', based on living 'crappily ever after'. Sure, we can agree to live a crappy life and say to hell with everybody, but, in reality, 'what goes around comes around'. You can trample over people and you can do whatever you want, but then you must be prepared and anticipate the karmic relapse. *Karma never forgets.*

It's impossible in a world of 7 billion people and counting today, that one can have an interaction with another without bringing karmic accountability into the equation of life. Nothing happens in life without accountability.

The basic law of karma (and also according to Isaac Newton) is that that every action has an opposite and equal reaction. For instance, if somebody is having three beefsteaks a day, washing them down with a bottle of scotch, and he's got the tablets to get rid of the cholesterol, he thinks he's ahead of the game. But, it's been researched that those very pills can increase his diabetes risk by 30 per cent. Once the diabetes kicks in, the erectile dysfunction kicks in, too. I've been in the pharmaceutical business long enough to tell the truth. Why am I sharing it? It's because I want to reach out to you.

I don't want to see anyone six feet under years too early, as long as I've had the chance to communicate with them. Communication is from the Latin word *communicare*, simply to make knowledge common to all for their benefit. I'm also not a hard-hitting educationalist, because even *the word education* comes from the word *educere*. This means to 'bring out' that which already exists within you. This book aims to 'bring out' *your original God-given qualities, and for you to excel in life accordingly.*

We are all born in the image of God. What does it mean? You're still unique in the way you look amongst 7 billion-plus people, but there is something intrinsic in you, a code given to you when you were born, and those are our God-given original qualities of Peace, Love, Truth, Power, and Bliss. An enlightened education brings out those original values that you were born with. We find in life those original values are suppressed by the acquired negative qualities which are predominant in human nature today.

Why is the current state of the world very negative? Simple. It's the law of entropy. Entropy is a measure of the number of specific ways in which a system may be arranged, often taken to be a measure of disorder. We, the human race, currently driven by fear as opposed to love, have collectively amassed enough arms and ammunition—the specific firepower—to physically kill every human being 11 times over. Our so-called leaders with power have enough 'lead' power to annihilate the world. What need is there for that? Overkill indeed.

The world over is in this Age of Aquarius—an age of freedom. It is the era in which the great phenomenon of democracy will grow exponentially and the mental landscape is a free-for-all, in which people are driven by both their virtues and vices. It's no longer that Golden Age where we lived in truth, were driven exclusively by virtues, were saturated with contentment, and only expressed and interacted with pure love, peace, and happiness.

You have to get back to that original blueprint that was given to you and then observe what is really going on in the world and your interactions.

I am what some call a man of the world. I've lived in so many countries and on so many continents that, basically, I'm now just a citizen of the world. The sharing is to impact a complete spectrum of people, because I consider that everyone is a CEO of their lives. If you don't give enough respect to the individual, that individual is never going to respect you. Every CEO who wants to analyse everything in black and white has to remember that there's a massive grey area out there. That grey area is the grey matter of the brain; the grey matter that contains emotional and spiritual intelligence. You have to understand you cannot take an iron rod and knock it over people's heads and say, 'It's black and white.' If one is able to master understanding the grey matter of life, one is able to have mastery over human resources, which are the golden capital of any organisation worth its salt.

GEMS FROM THE OCEAN OF WISDOM

'The Key is: All is contained in the soul. The Brain is the organ which acts as a screen for the soul to project onto and activate the body.'

'Grey Matter / Grey Areas of life are dispelled when the original brilliance of the soul is able to shine through like a flawless diamond. We were all born in the likeness of God, full with all His original qualities.'

—RDM

'Accurate focus is through (1) willpower, (2) logic, and (3) the heart of understanding. If you want only logic in my book, you're not going to find it. There's a massive amount of willpower, but remember that vision is a hundred times more powerful than willpower, and if you want to develop that vision, then you have to go deep into the heart of understanding.'

—RDM

When a palmist studies the palm of your hand, it is possible him to show exactly to how evolved, and balanced or unbalanced one is in this lifetime in terms of willpower, logic, and the heart of understanding. It's everyone's personal drive, once the willpower kicks in, to say, 'I will do this. Yes, I have enough logic to know what is right and wrong, and to make it black and white, but within that, I must develop a large and generous heart of under-standing.' This will generate accurate *holistic* focus on the way forward.

Even within the basics of palmistry, it can be shown that there are *some* people only cut out to enslave themselves. All they do is work, eat, sleep, and get back to work. That's all. That's according to their personal biological alarm clock. They don't have time for anything. They don't have time for *any quality* interchange or to even understand where they're going. In *The Seven Habits of Highly Effective People*, Steven Covey explained that these types of people are enslaved in the vicious cycle of Quadrant 1, 'urgent and important tasks', living their lives in the realm of constant 'fire fighting'. Such a life leads to the ultimate burnout, and at worst, over-loaded with prescription drugs to fend off the demons of high cholesterol, blood pressure, diabetes, and erectile dysfunc-tion, to name but a few.

So, as we 'walk through the valley of the shadow of death', who is guaranteeing our next minute? Are you going to sign in blood that I'm going to live the next minute? You can't. There are no guaran-tees. If there are no guarantees, then in this 'sudden death' world, let's vow to live life to the maximum, each and every moment of our lives. As the educator and businessman Stephen Covey said, this is the greatest thing that we can live with, when we can take stock of who we are, where we are.

I would say even your spouse is a CEO; your teacher is a CEO. Everyone is a leader of him or herself. There is nothing you can do in the Age of Aquarius to control people. If you have a controlling nature, and attempt to control another, in England, they would retort with a defiant, 'here's two fingers to you, mate', and in America, they would signal a curt, 'Up yours.' Little do people know that the 'two fingers' derogatory 'V' sign of these times stems from the battle of Agincourt (1415). The gesture was used by English archers in defiance of the French threat that any captured longbowmen would have their two bow-fingers cut off. *On a positive note, we also have situations when the very same bow fingers switched around 180 degrees to face the opposite direction are used productively to display the Winston Churchill 'V' sign for victory, or a 'V' sign for peace.* Later in the book, page 173, offers further enlightenment on the significance of these two fingers which in palmistry are also referred to as the fingers of Jupiter (Index) and Saturn (middle).

This book is given out with humility to the world. What I expect is that people will mindfully *mix and blend* the ideas and come out with a *fresh mindset based on their own experiences.* Those experiences will impact like a stone skimming and creating ripples over a clear blue pond. I believe that I'm pitching this book out because there's a difference between stone intellect and divine intellect.

Not everyone appreciates your gifts of wisdom. Some will even try to bring you down for trying to enlighten them. However, this must never deter one from sharing truth. Rest assured that the swans of humanity will be able to discern the pearls from the stones.

I want to share another little story with you. A king was walking in the fields one day. 'Why am I here seated on my throne and these people are toiling in the fields all day?' His wise counsel replied, 'Listen, this is exactly the way it is.' He says, 'No, I don't believe it. Let me chuck a few diamonds into the field.'

All those people were doing was just loading up the dirt into their baskets. They never even bothered to look to see whether the diamonds were there. All they did was just fling the dirt into their baskets as though it were any other day. It didn't matter.

In this book, you will find there are some real diamonds that people are going to pick up, and put it in their inner treasury. Yet, the worst thing is having a treasury and not sharing, not helping others with their treasures—whether real diamonds, or knowledge, which is more powerful than any form of money. An old Scottish proverb states: 'The real measure of your wealth is how much you'd be worth if you lost all your money.' The knowledge of truth is indeed priceless and imperishable.

There is another famous saying, attributed to a variety of people, including Brooke Astor: 'Money is like manure.' If you don't spread it around, you don't fertilize anything. If it remains with you, locked up, it starts to stink. Even if you have the gems and diamonds within, if you don't share them, they have no value. That is my number-one goal for this book and what I want you, the reader, to get out of it. The paradox is that original virtues, when 'shared' (divided), become geometrically multiplied, making for a better world for us and all those around us. The Creed song 'Hide' says, 'divided is the one who dances, because the soul is so exposed'. It is said that when love is shared (divided), it becomes multiplied. This is the same when sharing all the virtues. One's life becomes an abundant garden of the best fruits for always.

THE PARADOX IS THAT ORIGINAL VIRTUES, WHEN 'SHARED' (DIVIDED), BECOME MULTIPLIED, MAKING FOR A BETTER WORLD FOR US AND ALL THOSE AROUND US.

I've spoken to CEOs of massive organizations who complain bitterly about fragmentations in their companies and differences and ego clashes. I know of two recent incidents of people, at the age of 40, slumping over their desks and dying. Why? These are people who are aggressively focused and driven physically and mentally, but they suppress their emotional and spiritual quotients. Imagine someone slumping over his or her desk. There's no value or quality in that life. In the modern era, we have seen this happen to bloggers who have died at their computers, literally from mental and physical exhaustion.

A simple question posed to gauge one's degree of understanding is, 'When one is both busy and thirsty, what does one do?' Many, in today's world, continue in their busyness until they die of 'dehydration'. An over-busy executive who makes no time for a silence break, the oxygen for the mind, and the water of knowledge to fulfil his soul, is heading for a burnout, like Elton John's famous 'candle in the wind'. *The human mind is so complex, and thoughts can be so scattered, that at times, the contents of the human mind can be likened to dry sand.* How can one organize *dry* sand? It's impossible to build a sandcastle just with *dry* sand. Water (the symbol of knowledge) is required to bind the sand together so it can be shaped by our hands.

CHAPTER 2

BACKGROUND

WHO IS RAJ?

y family's pharmaceutical company has been in West Africa for the past 53 years and has seen its fair share of trials and tribulations. I was born in India and lived there with my mother and younger brother until the age of 6. I hardly saw my father, as he was working abroad during my early years. For all the years and quality time I spent with him, he gave me an invaluable foundation and wealth of his experience and wisdom. He taught me, 'You can go to the depth of any ocean and find what's there, but you can never fully fathom what goes on in the depths of the human mind.'

His view on business was always focused on putting the OM back into commerce—to constantly have an 'abundance mentality', as he visualised business to an endless ocean. 'Go to the seashore', he would say, 'and have the courage to put your face in the sea and drink as much as you can; only then will you realize that it is an unlimited ocean.'

In commerce, there are those who exploit virtues, and those who exploit vices to generate their livelihood. The worst 'hood' is falsehood. In the Golden Age, before paradise was lost, we had kings with a divine intellect; however in today's Iron Age, we have two types of kings—those with a stone intellect, and those with a divine intellect. The key is to focus on the Light within all and expand that for the profit (good) of all.

On being decisive, my father said the world is about 'yes' or 'no'; there's no such thing as 'maybe'. The moment one takes responsibility, one becomes a leader, and then accountability is clear and personal. Finally, 'Indeed, it is said that music blows the dust of the soul, but regarding musical choice, or one's taste in music—be aware that one man's tonic is another's poison.'

> *'There is a great man who makes every man feel small. But the real great man is the man who makes every man feel great.'*
>
> —G. K. CHESTERTON

When I was 6 years old, I spent three years at school in Liberia, West Africa, and from age 9 onwards, I had my primary, secondary, and tertiary education in England at British boarding schools. I was fortunate to have a Scottish guardian, a man who worked with Boots, the blue-chip British pharmaceutical company, for 44 years. He became a close friend of my father and my second dad in the UK. His wife was Dutch, and became like a second mom to me. As a result, I also have a half-sister and half-brother who are Scottish-Dutch. It's a very multi-cultural experience.

In 1980, I graduated in England with a BA (Hons) in Business Studies, specializing in marketing. During my University years, my 'industrial training' year was a placement / internship with the British National Health Service, at a large Government hospital which was like a city unto itself. I did everything under the sun there, from being a porter, to day staffer with the girls in the office, to the major wards—including a cancer ward, to working with all the top administrators. A lot of people were quite astonished that I could cover the entire spectrum, but I was pretty much given access to all areas. Some were cautious about interacting with me, as they thought I was an undercover agent. I met the greatest administrators, doctors, pharmacists, nurses, and "ordinary people" performing their special roles in life, and experienced the biggest parties. I witnessed birth at the neo-natal ward, death at the morgue, and I was fortunate to be exposed to every facet of that hospital. All of it gave me a wake-up call as to what life was really about.

When I returned to my fourth and final year at University, I had a completely different perspective on how privileged I was to be studying, as opposed to working in the 'real world'. Out of my altered perspective on the complex nature the healthcare world emerged a deep self respect and self esteem for returning to the classroom. This new determination led me to fall in love with marketing (my final year specialisation), which still today I use in my business.

Being in the pharmaceutical business and having a deep respect and regard for all professionals in the organization, I got to a point where people would sometimes refer to me as doctor when I speak about pharmaceuticals. Maybe this is what gives me a different perspective, a holistic perspective as to what's happening… because I can see both the commercial and the ethical side of the pharmaceutical industry.

Throughout my 33 years in Africa after graduation, I've had a very 'broad spectrum' experience in the realm of pharmaceutical marketing. There was a time when we represented almost every prime multinational pharmaceutical company in the world, selling over one thousand 'specialties' under one roof. From the life-saving specialities which healed, to preventative medicines that maintained good health, to the products which were open to abuse.

For example, products that were contraindicated for pregnancies sold in millions, as they were open to abuse to abort pregnancies. There was a product called Primodos, another Cumorit (by Schering), and Menstrogen-F (by Organon). Gradually, the World Health Organization (W.H.O.) became wise to the misuse and banned them all worldwide. Today, all of these products are still produced in back-street factories around the world, and are still available in third-world markets for mass abuse. There's another product that's currently being produced by Pfizer, namely Cytotec (Misoprostal) that is the current 'flavour of the month', being hugely misused in the market.

Once again, we return to the concept of 'ricochet effect'. What goes around comes around. The values with which we run the organization are very deep in self-management leadership. As much as people like a hierarchy, there's no way we can have the 'stick-and-carrot', donkey-drive type of ethic. It has to be a higher ethic that drives itself, and that drives the overall organisation.

According to the current trend in motivational leadership principles, a multitude of varying motivational theories will emerge and reach worldwide recognition, all based on the sharing of personal experiences. Personal experience and taking responsibility are the greatest teachers in the world. Everybody has a story. Even with the most introverted, seemingly uninteresting people, if they have reflected on their original values and experiences, and are allowed to share them, can pleasantly surprise us. The best and most effective leadership principles are best expressed by people who are driven by the original qualities of the soul: truth, peace, love, happiness, and bliss.

THE SWEET ANAESTHETIC OF EGO: "LET ME REST FOR A WHILE, ALL WILL BE OK..."

There's a poem called *Ozymandias*. When my son, then aged 13, read it to me, I was struck by the fact that it sounded like 'Oh, See Man Dies'—it's about a famous pharaoh who conquered what he thought was the whole world, and boasted on the stone inscription, 'Look on my works, ye mighty, and despair.' And yet, now the mighty Ozymandias is nowhere in sight. Nothing remains around the decay of his arrogant statue, except his two legs and the remains of his egotistical head: 'On the sand, half sunk a shattered visage lies, whose frown, and wrinkled lip, and sneer of cold command'. The rest of it has crumbled and decayed.

Man dies after all. Today, you can insure the body for physical death, and those in your will can benefit from the physical monetary 'payout'. However, can you insure your soul? Like Ozymandias and his infamous statue, our physical bodies will also one day turn into 'dust to dust', and 'ashes to ashes'. What good is a 'frown, wrinkled lip, and sneer of cold command' going to do for Ozymandias, or for us, in our next incarnation, the hereafter? The leadership principles that you work on must be guided by the original qualities you were born with, and target on achieving the imperishable treasures that life offers. This ensures you are paying your premiums towards insuring your soul. It will assist you in navigating through all facets of life accurately, guided by the inner compass of truth within the landscape of the mind.

I believe there is a blueprint, which, if studied carefully, will help people to see themselves in a new paradigm, a much clearer light, which will always help to guide them through life with the right choices. 'No matter what your faith may be, it's the universal light of God that drives everyone.' The aim is to release your original being, the self-sovereign, the hero, the leader within.

THE YOGA OF HUMANITY—THE PATH TO PEACE

When there are harmony and stillness within, I can hear the voice of my own original inner wisdom. In union with our 'God-self', we enter into the realm of safety and security, and experience a sense and exhilaration and achievement.

This concept is the foundation of the Yoga of Humanity. My level of happiness, peace, and bliss is based on consciousness, and my consciousness is based on my state of 'Being', as opposed to my state of 'Doing'.

In Andrew Marvell's poem, *A Dialogue Between the Soul and the Body*, there is an argument between the two. The spirit feels shackled by the body's arms and legs, whereas the body complains that it feels like a house, a prison cell, that has been cursed and is haunted by a ghost—the spirit.

Indeed, we have sperm cells, which ultimately create blood cells, body cells. Cells are also prisons. Nowadays, we even have cell phones which steal our attention and lock our awareness. Once jailed, we lose sight of other realities in our lives. In Elizabethan times, the word *jail* was spelled as *gaol*. We also remain trapped in our physical cells, targeting our limited goals within the jail framework of our limited lives. When we sin—literally 'miss the target' or 'miss the point' in our lives—we remain imprisoned in the cell of our limited consciousness.

This form of yoga of the mental landscape can be likened to the art of photography, whose literal meaning is 'writing with light'. We need to access the point of light within, link with the Supreme light above, and then interact with others as points of light, thereby creating our fortune by 'writing with light'. This ensures we tread lightly, and shine 'white light', respecting the transient 'trustee' nature of our true existence. We become decisive, and are able to play the part of a hero actor in all our roles on the drama stage of life, without getting entangled in any one role by 'over-acting' in it, thereby ensuring harmony. This can be likened to Sting's heartfelt promise in 'Fields of Gold', 'In the days still left, I swear, we'll walk in fields of gold . . .'

Humans do not need to belong to a specific religion in order to have a sense of moral right or wrong. In my view, moral rectitude is our natural original nature. Unfortunately, the mistaken idea that humans cannot be good without belonging to a specific religion is one that is dominant in most societies across the world. All religions are intrinsically founded on *Bhakti*— pure devotion for God. However, the map is not the journey, which we all have to make on our own. Throughout *our* journey in the cycle of life and time, the only permanent and faithful companion is *Truth*. Once we become enlightened to this, we never fear solitude, as the power of Truth fills our consciousness.

HUMAN BEINGS CAN ACHIEVE MORAL EXCELLENCE WITHOUT BELONGING TO A RELIGION, AS LONG AS THEY HOLD ON TO TRUTH.

Consciousness is everything—we do not need to be dependent on any one specific religion to care for ourselves, children, parents, family, friends, community members, and the aged. It is not being religious that makes us humanitarian. Doing good is natural to humans, not supernaturally induced. Human beings can achieve moral excellence without belonging to a religion, as long as they hold on to Truth, and use the inner compass of 'True North' to pilot their journey, to ensure they sow the seeds of greatness to reap the treasures of an immortal existence over the cycles of their many lives.

'When I do good, I feel good. When I do bad, I feel bad, and that is my religion.'

— ABRAHAM LINCOLN

In an interview, General Norman Schwartzkopf was asked if he thought there was room for forgiveness towards people who harboured and abetted the terrorists who perpetrated the 9/11 attacks on America. The general said, 'I believe that forgiving them is God's function. Our job is to arrange the meeting.'

In yoga, what is important is the meeting with our original being, which allows us to connect accurately with God—it is in this subtle, spiritual union that we are absolved of any wrongdoings.

Because of the dense undergrowth about their roots and trunks, in order to grow, the African palm tree has to climb high to reach the air and sunlight. By the time it reaches the light, it becomes weak and unstable, covered in parasites. The intense labour of harvesting the fruit makes it unproductive, leaving very poor those who depend on the fruit for their existence. However, when man clears the undergrowth ensuring that the surroundings of the palm tree are left clear and free, the tree is able to grow sturdy and strong in a shorter time, and the fruit is more easily and economically reached. Hence, nature ensures that the tree, fruit, and farmer all flourish.

Once the undergrowth of vice, superstition, suspicion, and dogmatic thought patterns is cleared away from the current mental landscape, our characters are able to flourish in the clear divine light of truth and sincerity. Then one can truly expose the inner polished diamond to live a life of brilliance for the self and all those we interact with in this great drama of life.

Those who lead must be eager to serve. True leaders are not those who ask first for assured positions of authority. Instead, they create opportunities for work, guided by the significant needs of their day. It is to them that the gates of genuine opportunities for leadership will open, giving entrance to a fair inheritance.

Truth expressed in words is real knowledge. Truth practised in daily life ensures accuracy, clarity, transparency, and honesty in actions (karma). Honesty in action is *Sukarma*—positive karma. Dishonesty in action is *Vikarma*—negative karma.

You are a product of your own thoughts, and thoughts are the seeds of our actions.

The aim is to focus on and perform righteous actions. Khalil Gibran enlightens us: 'When you love, you should not say, "God is in my heart", but rather, "I am in the heart of God."' This is reiterated by Abraham Lincoln's comment: 'Sir, my concern is not whether God is on our side; my greatest concern is to be on God's side, for God is always right.'

Integrity is defined as strict adherence to a moral code, reflected in transparent honesty and complete harmony in what one thinks, says, and does. It includes incorruptibility, sincerity, honour, and probity. In short, it is a measure (ME.SURE) of the quality of a person's character.

In order to succeed in today's world, one has a choice, either to:

[1] GET 'ON'—
cut corners (i.e. take short-cuts)

or

[2] GET HONEST

or

[3] GET HONOURS—
excel in life

Honesty, today, is a word that has lost its potency. Dishonesty is so pervasive that, at times, people cannot even trust their own family members. This is the Rust of Mistrust reflecting the current vicious cycle of Iron Age versus the virtuous cycle of the Golden Age.

Dr. Martin Luther King urges us to 'accept finite disappointment, but never to lose infinite hope'.

Hope is a rope that swings you through life.

GEMS FROM THE OCEAN OF WISDOM

'Hope is the companion of power, and mother of success; for who so hopes strongly has within him the gift of miracles.'

One is always driven towards earning a physical income. Acquisition and inculcation of spiritual knowledge is earning an imperishable income. Like a milk churn that makes butter by constantly shaking and turning milk or cream, one must churn on the knowledge and crystallise it to earn an imperishable income. This income will determine your outcome in life. Churn the knowledge and make it your own. That which is Internal is Eternal.

> *'Experience is not what happens to you; it is what you do with what happens to you.'*
>
> —Aldous Huxley

Elisabeth Kübler-Ross (author, psychiatrist), who studied terminal illness patients, published her groundbreaking book, *On Death and Dying*, in 1969. The book outlines the five stages that dying patients experience: denial, anger, bargaining, depression, and acceptance. Psychiatrists and social workers use this book extensively today to enlighten and bring reconciliation to the distraught minds of those who have lost loved ones and encounter a similar pattern of experience as terminally ill patients. We are enlightened that 'Death is the final stage of growth.' This is what it means to 'Die Alive'—to be 'Born again'. Keep burying yesterday, yester-moment, yester-second, and keep growing—have the potency to merge everything that has passed and allow the original diamond within to emerge.

GEMS FROM THE OCEAN OF WISDOM

'When there is harmony within myself, I can live in unity with others. The vision of a better world can then be made real.'

You can only give another person love, peace, and happiness, if you have first given the same to yourself. You cannot give those things to another person if do not possess them yourself. The key is to be merciful to yourself.

People pray or cry out to God, 'Why won't you be merciful?' Actually, God is tapping you on the shoulder, saying, 'Look, you have the knowledge. It's your move.' This requires us to cross over the bridge of *Bhakti* (pure devotion) into true knowledge. When you have this knowledge, these principles are based on those original qualities and positive values which are already blue-printed inside of you. They only have to be excavated and naturally emerge.

It is in performing righteous karma (actions), which are imperishable, that you ensure your soul for the next birth. Why is a king born a king and why is a pauper born in the gutter? It is to do with actions performed.

Think of Glenn Hoddle, once the England team football manager, who was sacked in 1999 for comments he made about people who were invalids, saying, 'Oh, it's a karmic thing.' They weren't angry with him when the England team lost at the World Cup, but when he was quoted saying disabled people were paying for sins committed in previous lives, it was too much. Many Britons, who had strenuously resisted the growing imposition of American-style political correctness, even conceded that the firing was a good idea. Hoddle, long known as a born-again Christian, was known to have 'somewhat unorthodox religious views'. 'You and I have been given two hands and two legs and half-decent brains,' *The Times* quoted him as saying. 'Some people have not been born like that for a reason. The karma is working from another time. I have nothing to hide about that. It is not only people with disabilities. What you sow, you have to reap.' The quote created an instant scandal, and led to his being fired.

He is one of the most famous British footballers, and wasn't one to get drunk and gamble with the boys. It didn't matter that Hoddle had long been a supporter of several organizations for the disabled. To be fair, though, said columnist Matthew Parris in *The Times*, the English 'should consider for a moment the insulting views to which some of our own politicians' differing faiths lead them. Some Ulster Protestants believe the Pope is an agent of the Devil. At least Hoddle was not imputing wickedness to any living person or proposing to hurt them.' Said one 'forgiving', handicapped Londoner, 'He spoke without thinking. You just take it with a pinch of salt.'

If it's a democratic world, let people have their say. When referring to the 'handicapped', let's refer to the heroism of Helen Keller, in reversing her karma, how she valiantly sowed the seeds to make the best use of her life. She contracted an illness which left her both deaf and blind before her second birthday, and yet she earned a Bachelor of Arts degree, became an author, political activist, and lecturer in her lifetime. Today, Helen Keller's wisdom is used to influence millions in the world of business and life.

Here are three of Helen Keller's golden thoughts:

> *'The only thing worse than being blind is having sight but no vision.'*

'It is wonderful how much time good people spend fighting the devil. If they would only expend the same amount of energy loving their fellow men, the devil would die in his own tracks of ennui.'

'Self-pity is our worst enemy, and if we yield to it, we can never do anything wise in this world.'

'Bring out the best in everyone.' At one time I had an alternative title for my book, called *Sunny Side Up*, because when I look at a person, I only look at the best that person has to offer. I know there's another side, perhaps a dark side, to everything today because we acquire so much negativity from the world, but how many of us have the ability to switch on that light within, and just walk around as a lighthouse? We should strive to be a beacon for the self and for all those who come into contact with us. 'Whenever decisions are to be made, it is very important that such a beacon be present to light the room.' When a lighted candle is used to light another, it loses nothing, but the room and the atmosphere double in brightness.

GEMS FROM THE OCEAN OF WISDOM

'Virtue illuminates everything: it fills what is empty, heals what is sick, and settles what is troubled.'

This is, again, a leadership principle to be light and live life like a carefree emperor. The key is to be careful; to be carefree, but never to be careless. I will refer to President Bill Clinton's moral slips. Be carefree, but not careless. The Lewinsky scandal was a political sex scandal that emerged in 1998, from a sexual relationship between United States President Bill Clinton and a 22-year-old White House intern, Monica Lewinsky. The news of this extra-marital affair and the resulting investigation eventually led to the impeachment of President Clinton in 1998 by the U.S. House of Representatives, and his subsequent acquittal on all impeachment charges of perjury and obstruction of justice in a tense 21-day Senate trial.

The scandal was variously referred to in the unforgiving and churlish tabloid press as 'Monicagate', 'Sexgate', and 'Zippergate', amongst many other names, following the '-gate' affix that had been popularised since the Watergate scandal.

There is strength in the adage 'Let sleeping dogs lie'—don't disturb them because your ego has been flustered. Again, Clinton had a build-up of good karma and good people who gathered around him and his family, praying and guiding them through their trauma. It is said, 'a family that prays together, stays together'. *A good leader must be careful and carefree, but any careless actions can make even the very best fall from grace.*

Again, Greatness is not about never falling down, but being able to rise up from the depths of hell, and prove your metal, which Bill Clinton certainly has done, and he tirelessly continues to perform good karma throughout Africa and the world. I was present at the YPO-WPO Global Edge in February 2014 when Bill Clinton was interviewed by Larry King. Currently, the Bill Clinton Foundation—the Clinton Global Initiative—has been responsible for building hospitals in Rwanda which provide values-based care, and aim to be self-sufficient by 2020. Also, during his term as president, he authorized hundreds of millions of dollars funding the human genome project and Nano technology project. Thanks to this initiative, today, the power of genomics can now sift out one in a billion cancer cells, and will one day soon completely cure cancer. Bill Clinton's credo is 'the power of cooperation and inclusivity will bring success', and stated that the late great Nelson Mandela's greatest move was to put his adversaries within his political parties to generate the power of synergistic cooperation.

'Some people think, "If I got humiliated in front of billions, I'd want to stick my head in an oven." I felt, "This is great—I can be who I am. I don't have to pretend anymore."'

— BILL CLINTON, ON OPRAH, AUGUST 2004

'If you live long enough, you will make mistakes. But if you learn from them, you will be a better person.'

—BILL CLINTON

'We are very blessed as a family. What will happen tomorrow I don't know; We just approach each day with the discipline of gratitude.'

—BILL CLINTON, FEB. 28, 2014 @ YPO GLOBAL EDGE ON THE DAY OF DAUGHTER, CHELSEA'S, 34TH BIRTHDAY

The Pentagon released a report in May 2013 highlighting a growing sexual assault epidemic staining the military. It estimated that as many as 26,000 military members may have been sexually assaulted in 2012, and that thousands of victims are unwilling to come forward, despite new oversight and assistance programs.

President Barack Obama urged U.S. Naval Academy graduates that this crime has 'no place in the greatest military on earth'. He also summoned military leaders to the White House and instructed them to lead a process to root out the problem.

'We need your honor, that inner compass that guides you, not when the path is easy and obvious, but when it's hard and uncertain, that tells you the difference between that which is right and that which is wrong,' Obama said. 'Perhaps it will be the moment when you think nobody's watching. But never forget that honor, like character, is what you do when nobody's looking.' Indeed, character is what you are, and how you behave when the lights are off. General Schwartzkopf defines a great leader as one who has both 'a good character and a strategy', but he further clarifies, 'If you have to let go of one, then leave the strategy and maintain your good character', which will see you through all the storms of current day life.

'Strategy has in it embedded the word "rat"— only good character will dispel the "rat" from any strategy to ensure genuine success.'

—RDM

JACKIE CHAN AND SPIRITUAL GROWTH

Whenever Jackie Chan in any of his movies faces an adversary or an adverse situation, he uses every single thing in his vision and reach as a weapon, be it a frying pan, a ladder, a bucket, or any other utensil. When I refer to the 'Jackie Chan of Spirituality', I mean that you should use every single moment for your own spiritual growth as if it were your last. It's good to be selfish about good things, because when you're selfish about good things, you hold on to them, use them for your benefit, and the good will overflow within your being. It can then be shared for the benefit of all you come into contact with.

The path of the yoga of humanity is basically a communion with your original being within. It's your body connecting with your soul and its original qualities. The mind yoga of humanity aims to enhance the quality of life, so you're more focused about the way you live and you experience life holistically.

The concept of rebirth and karma is also eloquently stated in the 'rock and roll' way by the 'Child in Time' by Deep Purple, who simply whisper, 'Wait for the ricochet.' What is that ricochet? That ricochet can happen any way, at any time in the cycle of life. You may think that you have trod on people, finished them off, yet life has a way of twisting things around. 'Whatever goes around comes around', is a well-worn motto which almost everyone is aware of. Alanis Morissette's rock classic 'Ironic' perfectly reflects the true irony of karma in this Iron Age.

Again, what I'm about to reveal to you, you already know. Yes, you know everything about the original values you were born with, because when you listen to them you hear them, you feel them;

you will nod your head because your conscience, the heartbeat of the soul, will nod its head as you read the book. Your conscience will then *lighten up* from within and you will use it. I'm absolutely certain of that. This point reminds me of the billboard at Cape Town airport which states, 'Your soul will remember having been here before.' The brief experience of beautiful Cape Town definitely felt like a very pleasant déjà vu.

I hope through this story you are able to find the diamonds already within you: your own original values. No matter what walk of life you are from, whether you are the wealthy CEO of a billion-dollar company, or a humble shopkeeper, those positive inner values will then blend with your IQ and greatly enrich your life in every way.

CHAPTER THREE

IAM'S ENLIGHTENMENT

REM sleep, characterized by rapid eye movement, is the sleep phase when dreams occur. It is similar to the effect that psychotropic drugs such as Amitriptyline have, and are prescribed by psychiatrists accordingly. When people have a lot of demons in their heads (the illusions of *maya*—negativity) and they take that drug, it gives them a lot of REM sleep. So, in effect, the inner 'demons' are dispelled by having the REM sleep.

Rapid eye movement in early morning sleep can give you dreams you remember, so the moment you wake up, you think, 'Ah, thank God, that was just a dream.' But then you learn something from that dream because of the fear it created in you, and you now understand that the fear itself was false. It's like *maya*: falsehood, illusions. All around us right now, there are hidden opportunities embedded in our lives, but as we are not in tune or accurately connected to our inner being, we cannot see them. The word fortune is about creating your inner fortitude, and being in tune with your original being. Liken this to a radio which needs to be switched on, aerial extended, dial tuned in, and volume turned up.

Each problem has hidden in it an opportunity so powerful that it literally dwarfs the problem. The greatest success stories were created by people who recognized a problem and turned it into opportunity. More important than your current status is your current 'station' in life. Take stock of where your 'berth', your train, your physical chariot, has reached in life. You have to become 'stationary' in your mind and reflect deeply. Many want to be *re-elected* to office, to never leave their power base, but they've never taken the time to truly *reflect* within. Living a life with *'correct standards'* is far more important than one's *'standard of living'*.

Yoga and meditation are not complicated; they are just a means of teaching your mind to think in a different way. To understand something, you need knowledge, but to feel it, you need experience.

Now we are on the battlefield once again.

Iam gets shot in Afghanistan and enters the 'deep sleep'. It is in that 'deep sleep' when he goes into the dreamscape of Truth. Iam, like you, will be reborn.

> *'If one is lucky, a solitary fantasy can totally transform one million realities.'*
>
> —Maya Angelou

AL, ALPHA, THE ALMIGHTY BEING, NOW COMMUNICATES WITH IAM

And now, these are AL's words to Iam, our soldier, and our CEO.

'The journey is through time itself. The cycle of time is eternal, never ceasing. You were born in your birthday suit and will also physically die in the same birthday suit. However, the inner being, the soul imprinted with my original qualities, is eternal and can never die. This is your personal pilgrimage. You need the right *"pills" of enlightenment* in this *"grimm age"*.

'Your interaction with me is indeed your pilgrimage of remembrance. This will help you reflect deeply and make you into the spinner of self-realization. You will understand how the three aspects of time—yesterday, today, and tomorrow—are all merged and combined in this very moment. You will discover your true inner compass to navigate through life as a carefree emperor. Carefree, and always careful, but never careless.

'At this stage in the cycle I had no other option but to reveal everything to my children. As such is the state of the world today, pure gold is gold, but diamonds are even more precious. When you are fully aware of the entire garbage in this Iron Age that has clouded your intrinsic greatness with which you were born, then, and only then, can you dig deep within, and find and excavate the diamond that you truly are.

'Today's world is rife with the phenomena of GIGO (garbage-in, garbage-out). The water of knowledge, deep secrets, practical methodology, super-sensory experience through music which touches and blows the dust off the soul, and my unceasing eternal light upon you, will surely find your diamond within if, and only if, your inner seed is worthy of making the effort of internalising and absorbing all the truth which is being imparted to you.

'We can think of water as the symbol of knowledge. The font of wisdom is knowledge. Water accepts. It cleanses negativity, dirt, toxins, darkness, and dissolves all, leaving beauty and opportunity, the signs of learning and wisdom.

'When you are connected with me in humility, you will automatically experience constant cooperation from everyone. To become a carefree emperor, switch your consciousness from the perishable body to the imperishable soul.

'I will always simplify what seems complicated to you. It is a great paradox that simplicity comes from passing through many complex stages of learning.

'The word mantra means simply 'mind delivering'. It's basically whatever you stay busy with is what is energized. Where your focus is, that's where your energy flows.

'There are only two *maha-mantras* (Great Mantras) which you need to remember, internalise, and use in your life, in order to maintain a high level of consciousness. By spending every single moment at a high level of consciousness, your life becomes a celebration of joy, happiness, and strength.

'Use the mantra *Manmanabhav*, which simply means, "Submit your mind to me and me alone."'

'Use the mantra *Madyajibhav*, which simply ensures that you always "Keep your aim so you never sin."'

When you sin, you are simply "missing the target", or missing the point, and thereby creating waste. Become a trustee. Dissolve all waste thoughts. The formula for success is success equals effort divided by waste. *Achievement=Effort/Waste.* If you have the practice of having waste thoughts, you will deceive the self. Use the power of positivity to recycle and transform waste into the positive. Stay constantly positive, and use any external negativity to charge and power up your batteries. Remember, it takes both positive and negative connections to fully charge a battery.'

And these are the things that the Almighty told Iam. Our soldier. Our CEO.

What can we learn from just this, these early words on the battlefield?

The most comprehensive term for explaining *sin* is the Greek word *hamartia*, literally meaning 'missing the mark', as an archer's arrow would fall to the ground because it fell short of its target. We must learn to avoid waste, use the advice above, hit the targets to ensure success, and share this master blueprint of all motivational theories, the 'grand-daddy' of them all.

Andy Warhol once reflected that 'In the future everybody will be world famous for fifteen minutes.' There's going to be a proliferation of motivational theories in today's Aquarian Age, the age of freedom, an age which will witness an exponential global acceleration in the movement towards democracy, the age of a global mindscape which is a 'free for all', and in which 'freedom of expression' will become almost sacred for all.

As previously mentioned, our current mental landscape is full of the entire spectrum of virtues and vices, the foundation of how we act, interact, and behave in the world. I was present when the former British Prime Minister Tony Blair spoke on the platform of the Young Presidents Organization at the YPO-WPO Global Leadership Summit in Istanbul in March 2013. He remarked, 'Around the world, we need to understand democracy is not about a way of voting, but rather about a way of thinking. You cannot and must not politicize religion and thereby create a new oppression. When you take the lid off an oppressive regime, all sorts of ethnic tribal differences come to surface and can create chaos, which is incredibly difficult to manage. There's no such thing as an automatic shift from oppressive regime to democracy.'

Hence, we need to examine our mental landscape of virtues versus vices. *Experience* and *responsibility* are the greatest teachers. Sharing your experience is the greatest *communication*, whose origin is from the Latin word communicare, simply meaning to 'make common'. Sharing your experience with others is the best way to carry forward the legacy of the wisdom keepers in the world.

Another formula for success defines that success is based on (1) 10 per cent intelligence, (2) 20 per cent luck (which is also *'L.abour U.nder C.orrect K.nowledge*'), and finally, (3) 70 per cent what you learn from other people—wisdom and experience. You can't buy it—a good mentor is someone whose hindsight becomes your foresight.

Today, we have a million and one motivational theories born daily. Yes, a hundred new 99-cent motivational self-help books will have appeared by the time I have finished typing this sentence on my iPad.

It's similar to people's addiction to reality TV today. Everybody wants to share something and, again, sharing of experience is the greatest form of communication. That's why people are so addicted to real-life experiences being expounded on TV.

There is such a prolific worldwide demand for any variation of reality TV, and also for "mash-ups" which become manifest when two different tracks or genres of music are blended for a fresh musical experience, that human minds continue to toil tirelessly experimenting and creating more and more. If today, Vyasa, author of the *Bhagavad Gita*, had met Jonathan Swift, then we would probably have given birth to a book entitled *The* Kurukshetra *of Lilliput*, where a war raged between two kingdoms over a dispute about which is the correct end of the boiled egg to be cracked before it is consumed. *Kurekshetra* was the battleground upon which Arjuna was enlightened via Krishna. The King of the humble, oversized (60 foot tall) Brobdingnagians commented about miniscule Lilliputians (6 inches tall), 'I cannot but conclude the bulk of your natives to be the most pernicious race of little odious vermin that nature ever suffered to crawl upon the surface of the Earth.'

The Bhagavad Gita (The Divine Song) is technically referred to as *Smriti*, which is the sharing of remembered text, as opposed to *Śhruti*, which is believed to be direct revelation.

'When we talk about democracy and motivation, 'education makes a people easy to lead but difficult to drive; easy to govern, but impossible to enslave.'

—HENRY PETER BROUGHAM

True guidance is like a small lamp in a dark forest: it doesn't show everything at once, but gives the light for the next step to be safe.

PUTTING THE OM BACK INTO COMMERCE

Virtue in one's inner world is expressed as dignity in the outer world. The current mental landscape of 'virtues versus vice' gave rise to the birth and evolution of the democratic legal system, in attempting to control the so-called 'demons in crisis' within all of us. Of course, the problem is, there isn't one single system worldwide. Each democracy is different, and each country has its own legal system; but all systems have a singular focus—that is for a clear conscience to be champion and ensure that virtue triumphs over vice.

Jonathan Swift wrote, 'Judges are picked out from the most dexterous lawyers, who are grown old or lazy, and having been biased all their lives against truth and equity, are under such a fatal necessity of favoring fraud, perjury and oppression, that I have known several of them to refuse a large bribe from the side of where justice lay, rather than injure the faculty by doing anything unbecoming their nature in office.' There was an age in human existence when people were righteous, and there was never the need of a judicial system.

Shakespeare in King Lear noted, 'Plate sin with gold, and the strong lance of justice hurtless breaks. Arm it in rags, and a pigmy's straw doth pierce it.'

Khalil Gibran wrote, 'There exists in all of us a God-self, and a pigmy-self.'

'A lie can travel halfway around the world while the truth is putting on its shoes.'

—MARK TWAIN

When the mind is clogged, removing the 'clogs' involves having mercy on the self. 'Log in to' your inner self and 'log in to' the Supreme Being through whose design you were produced, and then 'log on to' the world. Experience the magical pyramid, the triangle of harmony. This action gets the 'cogs' moving in the mind. Remove the 'clogs' and those old logbooks of hatred are cleansed. When you are able to see the inner logbook clearly, you are able to become like Gibran's prophet, who in his realization of his fortune states, 'If this is my day of harvest, in what fields have I sowed the seed, and in what unremembered seasons?'

As a CEO, Iam had studied the concept of discovering and promoting 'Blue Ocean' products, and aggressively discarding the 'Red Ocean' products, which flounder in the blood-red ocean of dog-eat-dog competition. However, nothing in all his experiences prepared him for being personally flung into a black and bleak ocean.

Iam is flung into an ominous nightmare – a vivid imagining of the shark versus the dolphin. He visualizes he's deep in an ocean in the middle of nowhere, drowning, an analogy of his current state in reality. Together with the fear of drowning, the ocean is dark and full of terrifying creatures. Specific in his fear is the shark, again a reflection of himself in the real world. A shark aggressively approaches Iam and he senses, as in the business world, a 'shark attack', which he could easily counter and neutralize. But here in the depth of hell he has become distraught and helpless, knowing that it is his fate to be chopped in half and suffer excruciating pain and certain death.

At that split second, he repents, and an explosion of compassion emerges from his heart as he visually empathizes with all those whom he has wronged. A large dolphin emerges and swims circles around Iam. The circles are so fast that they create a tornado-like effect, keeping Iam safely in the 'eye of the storm', where he's able to withdraw into his inner being and find peace within the turmoil.

The shark retreats, but is still bloodthirsty and has to feed itself, regardless. It has no intellect compared to the gentle dolphin. The shark heads to attack Iam once again. The dolphin swiftly leaves Iam, who now delves deeper into the foundation of his faith and conscience, knowing that he had indeed been a replica of the shark in his egotistical world—his mind driven by ego, lust, and greed—and now he was awaiting the same fate to eat him out of his miserable existence. For all his wealth, he was indeed *miserable*, *able* only to be a *miser*.

Remaining detached from the surrounding chaos, he awaited his fate. A few seconds, which seemed like an entire lifetime, overwhelm him, flashing at the speed of light through all the corridors of his mind.

With this switch of consciousness, the dolphin moves swiftly into position, and at lightning speed, uses its snout to pierce the side of the shark. The blood gushes out of the shark, though the shark feels almost no pain as it focuses on its single-minded aim to consume Iam at any cost. As it approaches Iam, the blood drains out, leaving the shark completely weakened, and gradually its own weight drags it deeper into the ocean, far away from Iam.

Sharks are warm-bodied, and not warm-blooded like humans; they cannot maintain a perfectly stable temperature. They constantly feed on blubber-rich seals and whale carcasses, because they require about ten times as much energy to keep their bodies heated and warmer than the ambient water around them. The warm muscles allow the shark to venture much deeper into the colder waters of the ocean as it hunts for prey, and ensures the shark constantly maintains its explosive power. Sharks use their eyesight to hunt prey, and hence like to hunt when it is light out, though they do like conditions that are low visibility because they depend on stealth to track down their prey. When they open their jaws, their eyes actually roll back into their head to protect them—so they are actually blind when taking a bite. They are not as agile as their prey, who can escape quickly when danger is sensed. The shark's mortal enemy is the dolphin. The dolphin is faster, more intelligent, more agile, and has strength enough to kill a shark.

As a visionary, if you can perceive, you can achieve anything. Perceive, conceive, believe, achieve.

The Yoga of Humanity is the practice of being truly human, based on using the spiritual intellect (the SQ, the Spiritual Quotient) to clearly understand the voyage of the mind through the cycle of time.

Faith and conscience (the heartbeat of the soul) rest in the intellect. A clouded intellect will have a faith that fluctuates, and a conscience that goes to sleep. Conscience can never die. It just goes to sleep in many people. *However, when the conscience wakes up to the truth, and is aware of wrongdoing, it can be the cause of intense mental anguish.*

This is one of the key reasons many people can't sleep, are constantly tired, and can't face the world today. Hence, this is why, in the United States alone, the annual market for psychotropic drugs is worth around $300 billion. In an August 2013 BBC interview, Ruby Wax, the comedienne who had also suffered from depression, stated, 'Depression is death, but it's in a chair.' Her research exposed that mental illness globally will evolve as the *most prevalent* 'sickness', valued at trillions of dollars worldwide. Almost one in four persons suffer this globally. She further explained that it has nothing to do with show business, stating, 'My inside does not know what I do for a living, and that depression is episodic, just like herpes'. One must exercise self-regulation and mindfulness, since 'nobody treats us as badly as we do' (Ruby Wax). We need to be open and trained to listen to our inner voices. In developing this subtle art, it will become clear that we will listen to the voice of virtue, and weave it into our daily lives. Simultaneously, we will not be focused on the vices, ensuring that the inner wolves of vice and havoc are always at bay.

> *'Now, if we are going to overcome, we must begin inside. God always begins there. An enemy inside the fort is far more dangerous than one outside.'*
>
> —DWIGHT L. MOODY

THE TITANIC LIFE

This is a broad generalisation, but can give us an indication of the connection between Zodiac signs, nature, the elements, and negative intellect:

Capricorn, Taurus, Virgo—Earth element—Stone intellect

Aries, Leo, Sagittarius—Fire element—Frying pan intellect

Pisces, Cancer, Scorpio—Water element—Frozen ice intellect

Aquarius, Gemini, Libra—Air element—Egotistical intellect/Anaesthetic

Without accurate knowledge of the soul, the blueprint which animates us, the mind can be likened to an iceberg, frozen in time. Cold and fearful. Ninety per cent hidden under the surface. People are 'blindsided' about their reality, becoming a danger to themselves and to others in their lives. True knowledge can only be acquired if the mind is not preoccupied, either as a sizzling hot frying pan or frozen in myopia. The water of knowledge on a hot frying pan just hisses way, and a myopic iceberg mind lives frozen in fear, never able to see with the third eye of knowledge the disaster about to happen. Such is a Titanic life.

What is a Titanic life? It is basically when you're sailing along without really knowing what lies around you, and your mind is too frozen to listen to the truth. Some minds are so myopic and frozen that you simply can't get in there with any spiritual truths. You cannot enlighten them, as much as you try. As such, they're like a Titanic life waiting to happen. Something or another goes wrong, whether at home, in business, or in personal health.

And here again, AL will teach us, as he teaches Iam, our soldier, our CEO.

AL'S SOLILOQUY ON IAM'S ENLIGHTENMENT

AL is alpha. AL is the Almighty. AL can mean anything to anyone, in whom they find the truth and put their faith and trust in. AL can mean different things to different people. AL is wherever they find their personal mirror of truth and are able to access glimpses of the original peace, purity, love, and bliss, and thereby place their faith.

'You go to the house of God, but do you know who God is? Hi All, this is AL. You added the word "mighty" to my name and made me larger than life. I've had to come into your realm of consciousness at this time to accurately introduce myself to you. It may come to you as a surprise, but you're all my long-lost-and-now-found children. Are you surprised in actual fact that I made each and every one of you in my image? How? I simply added 'L'. I added the 'L' of love to AL and you became my "All".

'Well, I'm happy to say that I have now found those in the world who have been truly searching for me. There's no need to be too scientific or conduct empirical measurements to prove my existence. Just develop faith that I am now here.

'Get to know yourself and you will get to know me. Once you make that link, I will impart knowledge and you will have to make the effort to become knowledgeable of the truth. I will also help to develop your third eye, your divine eye of knowledge, for you to gain divine insight to see the truth and make you *trikaaldharshi*, which is the "knower of the three aspects of time", yesterday, today, and tomorrow all rolled into this single moment; such is the power of purity of this very moment, this moment called now.

'In the cycle of life, I've sent many special children, my chosen ones, through pure births such as the "Immaculate Conception". Still, human beings continue to misunderstand my messages through these messengers. They were sent down to remind humanity how to live with the original qualities that were instilled in all by me: unadulterated purity, peace, power, love, happiness, and bliss. Followers come after the birth of their religious leaders. Hence, that is their part in the great drama that is known as life.

'I thank all the messengers who have kept the flame of truth burning, but as the numbers grew and time progressed, human beings now remember the messenger but have forgotten the original message. For example, within Christianity, one of the basic beliefs is that Jesus taught the true meaning of love—that is, *"If someone slaps you on one cheek, turn to them the other also. If someone takes your coat, do not withhold your shirt from them."*

'Are you confused? Did you know that, in truth, love has nothing to do with bodies? True and unconditional love is eternal and imperishable. At this time, your mind may reject this fundamental truth, but only experience will teach you and take you to the next level. You asked one of my chosen sons to add a touch of hate to Rome, and he answered that he only knew how to love. Only when the truth is revealed that all of humanity is One, and that each of you is a reflection of your brother or neighbour, will you close your eyes in shame and pain in recognition of your myopic vision and small-heartedness.

'Today one of my new children was asked about this thing called "hatred" that is destroying the world today. This is one of my new children who is in a state of innocence and considers her present world as the golden age. When any soul is born in the physical world, it has to pass through the cycle of infancy, growth, maturity, old age, and death. Enlightened ones understand the inevitability of this process.

'However, there's also another cycle that every soul must progress through, and that is the ages of time. There are five ages to be exact: Golden, Silver, Copper, Iron, and Diamond. The Diamond age is the age of confluence, and the age of enlightenment.

'Those who have a true thirst for knowledge will definitely receive the ocean of knowledge from me, but you can only *receive that which you perceive.* So, you must develop the power of perception and insight. Perception is the pathway to realization (i.e. that is seeing with *real eyes*). When you realize, you see with your *real eyes*. In fact, this is the third eye, which is linked directly to the intellect of the soul. You can visualize it as a microscope which constantly observes all the information coming into the mind through the senses, while recording all the experiences housed in the faculty of the *sanskars*, which is the storehouse of all the experiences that exist within the soul. The storehouse of the *sanskars* is where our traits and habits accumulate.

'Let's focus on today's age. Why is it referred to as the Iron Age? It's because iron has taken over the entire existence of all. "Isn't it ironic?" Alanis Morissette asks in her song, and you have all the examples of the irony of life, people's experiences and expectations not being fulfilled. An era of chaos and discontentment. There is only one law that can explain all the occurrences in the song and that is the law of karma.

'As you sow, so shall you reap. War machines are iron, computers are iron, human souls are degraded and rusted, cars are iron, and inner structures of many buildings are iron and steel.

'What is the Iron Age all about? It's basically about materialism taking over our entire being, creating our dependence in it.

'People have to play their part in the drama. To develop true and resilient faith, always remember that you are my child, and all in the world are my children.'

That's AL's Soliloquy. It has something for us all to remember. And how does it relate to the matters at hand, for those of us reading this book?

VIRTUE OVER VICE

Virtue over vice is something everyone can relate to. To achieve a deeper insight into the functioning of the vices, we must become familiar with the personification of the vices. The CEO is able to see clearly how his behavioural patterns have led to destruction. With Iam, it is the bullet heading for his forehead, seemingly demanding respect, even though inanimate ammunition intrinsically has no respect for itself. In reality, it is as worthless as the empty shell it leaves behind.

There are also the illusions of respect, created by people who are almost split-personality caricatures of Dr. Jekyll, and the evil Mr. Hyde. While exposing a virtuous outward persona, internally, hidden by the shadows of their fame, they are driven by vices, as in the case of British television personality Sir Jimmy Savile, a contract BBC entertainer. He was well respected by generations, but upon his death, it came out that he allegedly molested hundreds of people, including prepubescent girls and boys, as well as adults. Scotland Yard established Operation Yewtree to continue investigating historical sexual offences after claims of abuse were made against Savile following his death at the age of 84 in 2011.

In this astrological Age of Aquarius, this is the current landscape of every mind in the world, and there's an unprecedented movement towards complete freedom, complete democracy, and complete knowledge.

There was a time we had only a noble mind, where we could only interact with virtue. However, at this time in the world cycle, and with the law of entropy, everything becomes degraded. Currently, our golden mind has been mixed with the alloy of the falsehood of vices. What I mean by degraded is we are completely aware of everything. We're aware of all the virtues and vices, and in terms of the personification of the vices, we used to be gold, but now we've become a shell. A shell is worthless like the 5-hells, which also contribute to unworthy action. The five hells are the vices of Ego, Lust, Greed, Anger, and Negative Attachment.

BUILDING CONSTRUCTED BY VICE

If we construct a building made with personification of vices, the 'five hells', we start with Ego at the top of the building, and Ego says, *'I know, therefore I control.'* On the next floor down is Lust, which says, *'I create and I possess.'* On the third floor, we have Greed. That is, *'My well is overflowing and full but I'm still very thirsty and I don't know why. I keep looking for fulfilment by grabbing whatever I can materially and I don't know why I'm not fulfilled.'* On the floor below is Anger. *'I expect, and if you don't perform I will get angry.'* That burns the whole of spirituality. The last and most subtle of these vices is on the ground floor, where we find Attachment. A lot of people think attachment is a good thing, but attachment is really love for selfish purposes. Attachment says, *'Mine and only mine, no one else allowed.'*

You are in a world, you're a transient being, you're passing through, and as such, you're a trustee—a trustee of your body, and of all the relationships given to you. That's the opposite of attachment, which is 'love' for selfish purposes, and which creates a lot of pain and the fear of loss.

5-storey building with an underground car park. The underground car park is representative of the sixth vice, which is Laziness. Laziness is the vice which intoxicates one to have a complete lack of zeal and enthusiasm. This is the underground opium of the masses, which saps all energy, leaving everyone lackluster.

5-storey building with an underground car park. The underground car park is representative of the 6th virtue of zeal and enthusiasm. Having constant zeal and enthusiasm zaps (energises) one to be constantly alert.

On the opposite side of virtues are the vices. The CEO is able to see the various negative behavioural patterns and realizes how ego has driven him: 'I know and therefore I control.' The vice of Ego has put a stranglehold on his heart and mind. Ego is like ether, a sweet anaesthetic that makes you think, 'Oh, I've got it right, because I'm always right, and everyone else is a fool.' Pethidine is a narcotic anaesthetic commonly used for conditions of extreme pain in terminally ill cancer patients, and also at times for victims of shark attacks. People who have had a leg bitten off by a shark, once anaesthetised by Pethidine, have almost no awareness that they are missing a leg. Such is Ego, a strong and sweet anaesthetic, which keeps you in the cocoon of your limited understanding of the actual truth. An egotistical person thinks he exerts control over others, but the moment his back is turned, all types of disrespectful abuse is hurled at him.

An egotistical person is delusional. The opposite of ego is deep humility, which has a deep self-respect and profound respect for others. When you exhibit humility, people will genuinely confide in you, which can be a great source of enlightenment. This,in turn, ensures that you reduce the chances of ever being blindsided in the journey of life.

So on the second stage is the strong, possessive vice of lust, whose personification states 'I create and I possess'. The vice of lust can be visualised as a selfish sculptor. You're sculpting the other human being, and if their finger is out of place, you literally want to break it. 'Who said you could move that', bellows Lust, 'because only I create and I possess!' It's all possessiveness and creation within a limited mind-set, again divorced from the truth. The vice of lust in its extreme form can be seen when referring to the case of Jimmy Savile, or others who have this lust drive 'creating and possessing' victims—who are young, impressionable, and easily led—as sex objects. Abusing them is like lighting a fire that destroys all spirituality.

On the opposite spectrum of lust is unconditional love. All of these virtues and vices are on a spectrum. The one who is lust-driven thinks he is expressing love. The one who is being egotistical knows he feels he's absolutely right, and he also feels he's humble, but it's not true humility. When you look into the heart of your soul—the conscience—you will know the truth.

So, all of these vices are also the doorways into illusion. For instance, Savile did what he did because he was driven by lust, 'I create and I possess'. He was loved by many, but in the end, even after his death, his headstone was pulled down and hundreds of victims came out and reported what he had done to them. It ruined everything he had achieved, even his 'honourable' program, 'Jim'll Fix It', a long-running BBC show that ran between 1975 and 1994. Savile encouraged children to write in to have their wishes granted. Savile would miraculously 'fix it' for the wishes of several viewers to come true each week. Eighteen years after the show ceased airing, allegations of child sex abuse were made, including claims that special episodes of 'Jim'll Fix It' were devised by Savile in order to gain access to victims.

The opposite of greed is negative attachment. The opposite of anger is tolerance. The opposite of negative attachment is a relationship of trusteeship for everything that you have in life.

THE DOORWAYS OF HELL

Hell is an illusion. One's entry gate into *maya* (or illusion) is being driven by the vices. Being driven by vices ensures that one will live and die an illusive life. One's exit gate out of that life of illusion is to live by the virtues, and of course, being fully aware and accepting that truth is your faithful and permanent companion throughout life. *It is truth which allows one to hold on to the imperishable versus falsehood, which focuses on only that which is perishable.* Vices make you as worthless as a shell. Virtues unravel your diamond self.

The Alchemist's greatest secret is that anything that is perceived as negative is only illusion *(maya)*.

> *'Real difficulties can be overcome. It is only the imaginary ones that are unconquerable.'*
>
> —THEODORE N. VAIL

The reason being that imaginary ones are, in fact, *maya* / illusion.

Great care must be taken, because the vices are all-powerful. Even if you conquered Ego, and Lust, and Greed, the amazing thing about these vices is that they have the ability to wake each other up, if even a trace remains. Even if you have attachment to something, attachment to a goal, attachment to some work you've done, attachment to the results, it's as bad as a gardener planting a seed and shooting a hose at the ground and saying, GROW! GROW! GROW! And it's so destructive. You get so attached to the result that if it doesn't work, then Anger can enter into play; Attachment wakes up Anger. If Anger doesn't work, it wakes up Greed; if Greed doesn't work, it wakes up Lust. If Lust doesn't succeed, it then wakes up the grand-daddy of all vices, Ego—which yells from the depth of its hollow ignorance, 'I know, therefore I control', getting high on its own anaesthetic, sinking deeper into falsehood.

All of these vices drive us daily. We demand respect within our world, our business world, our family world, but behind our back, we have no value and that is why, when the world starts crumbling around us, we wonder, 'Hey, I thought I had it all under control. What's happening?'

So, the key is to perform actions such that one never has to *demand*, but rather *command* respect. *When demanding respect*, somewhere down the line you will be 'blindsided', because your demands require much effort and attention from your subordinates, who will be prone to becoming exhausted by a demanding job. People require great patience and skill to deal with your endless demands. On the other hand, commanding respect is imperishable. It has legacy, and if you command respect, it's like you set up your future life. Commanding has the word 'om' in it. In commanding, one has a bird's eye view, like a commanding view of the ocean, literally being at or having a relatively great or specific elevation.

Metaphysically, this means you are able to have the complete picture, and interact with self-respect, confidence, and self-esteem, an overall sense of self-worth or personal value. Self-esteem is a personality trait, which means that it tends to be stable and enduring, and this, in turn, creates a ripple effect of positivity on all those around you.

You can insure your physical body, but can you insure your soul? That is why it is the very law of karma which determines whether somebody is born a pauper or a king, or someone is born with a good intellect or a dull intellect.

Choosing virtue over vice brings us to a diamond level. In today's age, virtue is corrupted by vice. When you open your eyes and ears to the news in the world, it is really very negative. Today's negative daily news bulletins are like bullets, perpetuating violence and harm within us. The news bulletin is the 'new' 'bullet' 'in'. Some of it is announced in a flash, a deluge of negative stories, of teenagers raping a girl because they're obsessed with online pornography, or a man putting his 3-month-old child in a microwave for 20 seconds. The current list of man's inhumanity to man goes on endlessly.

Those things make your mind go mad. There are spiritual principles which guide us such as 'Be aware, but not judgmental'—'see but don't see; hear but don't hear'. In other words, you have to be aware of all realities, but it is very important to maintain your sanity, knowing that the more garbage that comes in, the deeper you have to go to find that diamond within. It is a constant effort to stay truthful to yourself and truthful to your original being, and drive yourself in the outer world.

'The price of freedom is eternal vigilance.'

—THOMAS JEFFERSON

Jefferson was referring to vigilance over elected politicians—the need for citizens to vote and keep their eyes wide open, to ensure that the demon of extremism or self-interest (of whatever stripe) does not overthrow the fragile flower of democracy. This equally applies to the values of the soul. The company you keep colours you and tells you something is right, even though you know it's wrong. This requires an extra effort of consciousness. But it's a daily effort to remind yourself to hold on to imperishable truths in order to keep the balance. Darkness is everywhere; the point of light is tiny. One has to remain eternally vigilant, and focused.

'Good people do not need laws to tell them to act responsibly, while bad will find a way around the law.'

—PLATO

VIRTUES / VICES SPECTRUM

ORIGINAL QUALITIES	ACQUIRED QUALITIES
1 HUMILITY	EGO
2 LOVE	LUST
3 TOLERANCE	ANGER
4 CONTENTMENT	GREED
5 TRUSTEESHIP	ATTACHMENT

GEMS FROM THE OCEAN OF WISDOM

'Sometimes in life we wear so many masks that it becomes difficult to see our true selves.'

'Accepting the self and others unconditionally allows everyone to remove their masks and feel at ease with who they are.'

'Detaching myself from the roles I play will help me to get in touch with the part of me that is not an act.'

CHAPTER FOUR

BEING TRUE TO ONESELF

W e are aware of the biblical 'Sovereignty of God' and the 'Divine Right of Kings', the medieval idea that God had bestowed earthly power on the king, just as God had given spiritual power and authority to the Church.

True leadership, or sovereignty, starts with the self. There are precedents, perhaps even more disconcerting, within the fabric of the royal family; for example, King Edward VIII and Mrs. Simpson are real-life examples of fidelity and infidelity, and how much better one is when true to oneself.

Time magazine provided an exposé of what really goes on when someone chooses the path of infidelity. I've coined this as S.A.R.A.H.S. to make it easy for people to remember. The exposé looked at why people drift into infidelity. First is for better S.ex. The second letter 'A' is because they feel more A.ttractive in the company of another. Third, they feel more R.espected in the company of another. The fourth, A.nger at the spouse or lover. Fifth, H.abit. In habit, of course, if you remove the 'h', you have 'abit' left'; if you remove the 'a', 'bit' is left; if you remove the 'b', 'it' is still there; remove the 'i', and 't', the 'thought' is still there. So, a lot of people are unfaithful out of habit. The final one is for S.piritual reasons, which means we are searching for someone who is a soul mate. Understanding the mechanics behind S.A.R.A.H.S. perfectly covers the entire spectrum of how we are driven physically, emotionally, mentally, and spiritually.

THE DIFFICULTY OF BREAKING BAD (OR GOOD) HABITS

- *H.A.B.I.T.*

- *A.B.I.T.........REMAINS*

- *B.I.T...........REMAINS*

- *I.T.............REMAINS*

- *T...............THE THOUGHT or TRIGGER (STILL) REMAINS, and the SPARK of Habit can be re-ignited by any specific trigger*

'Thoughts become Words. Words become Actions. Actions become Habits. Habits become Character. Character becomes Destiny.'

—FRANK OUTLAW (CREATOR OF BiLo STORES USA)

'Habits are like a cable. We weave a strand of it every day and soon it cannot be broken.'

—HORACE MANN

Within the phrase 'S.A.R.A.H.S.', we have the entire spectrum from the basic physical sex to the highest level, a soul mate. All of us crave a soul mate, because we have already established that 'a love-filled relationship is the deepest desire of the human soul'. S.A.R.A.H.S. also covers the spectrum of Virtues and Vices: At one end of the spectrum we have love, and at the other end we have lust. So even if someone strays only for better sex, they do get burnt out anyway. They end up hurting each other, because invariably you cannot have just a sexual approach that is lust driven. That will always lead to some level of physical and mental burnout.

Shree Rajneesh (Osho), the late Indian guru and spiritual leader, in his broad collection of varied teachings, emphasized the importance of meditation, awareness, love, celebration, courage, creativity, and humour. However, he most infamously advocated a 'wide-open' attitude towards sexuality, a stance which earned him the title of 'sex guru' in the press. A BBC exposé stated that Rajneesh encouraged his followers to participate in 'free sex' (which gained him much popularity in the West), with the aim of draining themselves of their physical sex drive, and thereby being able to switch their consciousness towards God.

Rajneesh failed to take note of the *Sanskars* (the 'resolves' in the map of our soul), the tape recording that goes on within. The more one performs physical sex for the sake of more sex, that lust drive becomes part of habit, and in turn makes one dysfunctional. So a lot of people do things, and after so many years, they don't know why they're even doing it. Take the chain smoker. He doesn't know how the next cigarette got into his hand. Or the drunk who needs to go to Alcoholics Anonymous. He doesn't know why he polished off those two bottles of vodka. It does become a habit. So, it is with such physical relationships which can lead to sex addiction. People get deeper into their habits, and those who feel they have been used as a physical object feel unloved. They deny the heart, the mind, and the soul.

GEMS FROM THE OCEAN OF WISDOM

'As I do, so I become. Every action that I perform is recorded in me. These imprints and habits ultimately mould my character and destiny.'

The world is dying of a metaphysical version of AIDS and it has to do with A.ddictions, I.ntoxications and D.ependencies at a deeper level. You can get physical AIDS, but you can have a thing called mental AIDS, where addictions, intoxications, and dependencies have a stranglehold on you.

One has to understand the Blueprint and Heartbeat of the Soul, one's Inner Driver.

PRINCESS DIANA, PRINCE CHARLES, AND INFIDELITY IN THE PUBLIC EYE

A French proverb states, 'Marriage is a town besieged. Those within want to get out and those without want to get in.'

Former U.S. vice president Al Gore also commented, 'After marriage, husband and wife become two sides of a coin; they just can't face each other, but they still live together.'

This mirrors the dilemmas and challenges faced in the love triangle between Prince Charles, Lady Diana, and Camilla Parker Bowles.

To dispel the grip of S.A.R.A.H.S., one must commit to the FACTS:

F.AITH
Be faithful to fulfilling each other's needs.

A.CCOUNT
Be accountable—understand Karma—as you sow so shall you reap—holy matrimony—pyramid of harmony—purity—clarity, transparency, and honesty.

C.OMMIT and C.OMMUNICATE

Be committed and communicate with your mate—physically, emotionally, mentally, and spiritually.

T.RUST and T.OGETHERNESS

Trust one another together in solving all problems—the synergy of trust and togetherness is the most powerful, as 1+1 = 11.

S.OUL CONSCIOUSNESS

Keep God alive in your relationship with your spouse / keep the spirit alive. Soul-conscious beings (aware of their 'God-self', as described by Khalil Gibran) are 'thin skinned', i.e. those with a conscience which is 'alive and kicking', unlike 'body-conscious' beings (unaware of their 'God-self'), who are 'thick skinned', with a conscience in constant slumber, living in the realm of their 'Pygmy-self'.

> *'Growing old is mandatory;*
> *growing up is optional.'*
>
> —CHILI DAVIS

Only God keeps a register of every soul's interactions, and has a clear picture of the level of purity (truth), and appropriate / reciprocal level of impurity (falsehood) in each soul. Being true to the self, to God, and to others ensures dissolution of impurities, and settlement of past karmic debts and negative sanskars, and recalls the original purity within.

It has been said that Lady Di was so driven in her purity and desire for that love-filled relationship within the family that she then used that energy to take it worldwide. That is why, when she died, the amount of the outpouring of worldwide love for her was so strong and remains so today. What she gave out to the world is what was returned multi-million fold. Having come full circle, the seed of love will flower.

Even today, Princess Diana is the deceased celebrity many Americans would want to bring back to life, according to a *Vanity Fair* survey conducted about mortality released in October 2013. Some 35 per cent of people said Princess Diana, who died in a car crash in Paris on August 31, 1997, is the celebrity they would pick to bring back to life, compared to 14 per cent for Apple co-founder Steve Jobs, and 11 per cent for pop stars Michael Jackson and Whitney Houston. The nationwide telephone poll has a margin of error of plus or minus 3 percentage points.

Another relationship that elicited strong public reaction and threatened to cause a constitutional crisis in the United Kingdom and the Dominions was that between King Edward VIII and (his mistress) Mrs. Simpson (a commoner who had two living ex-husbands). Mrs. Simpson was determined to marry the king at all costs, in an almost militarily strategic operation, well documented in *The Art of the Strategist: 10 Essential Principles for Leading Your Company to Victory* by William A. Cohen.

Cohen concludes that the essential principles can be used successfully to perform positive or negative actions, and achieve the desired aim, even if it's Machiavellian. However, the law of karma will be the final settler, and in the end negative achievements will be short-lived; only the positive will stand the test of time and survive.

All of these relationships have their repercussions, as in King Lear (which is an anagram of 'REAL'), losing touch with the reality of royalty and self-sovereignty and thereby performing off-target unrighteous actions.

The egotistical King Lear demanded respect from his three daughters, and was fooled by the two elder sycophantic daughters. They massaged his ego, and prompted him to banish the youngest innocent daughter, thereby releasing the power of the kingdom into their malevolent hands. Lear is, to his shock, rudely banished from his own kingdom by those 'pelican (bloodsucking) daughters'. The lightening bolt of his self-realization comes when he is flung out in the world, tormented. The Bob Dylan song, 'Like a Rolling Stone', would reverberate well in describing and questioning Lear's cathartic predicament.

We have to look at King Lear as an example for ourselves as well. When you lose what you have, and you're thrown out into the world, that is when you start reflecting into your inner world and start to *realize*, or see with *'real eyes'*, what's really going on. It takes you back to your original kingship. It's about making the effort in one's inner mindscape to traverse through a cathartic process, to purify oneself, to return to the truth.

There's a massive thunderstorm and Lear is out in the marshlands suffering, which is similar to the mental landscape of anyone experiencing the trauma of a bad decision, whether king or humble peasant, whether CEO or factory worker, traversing through their inner anguish, which, when accepted positively, only works in enlightening them that there's something deeply wrong. The pupil is ready and the teacher has appeared. It's time when they have to reassess and re-engineer their thinking. Lear lost touch with what is real; hence, he has to experience the trauma, the madness, which takes him back to that which is real.

We all need to be clear about our ultimate destiny. Let us begin with the end in mind so that we are clear about the consequences of all our actions to ensure we leave behind a worthy legacy.

There's a play of words in that 'tiredness comes from over thinking', the *thin king*. *Thin King* is a *miserly king*. Over-thinking (worrying) about everything he has to do, rather than simply doing it. A thin king is not royalty. U2 would say, 'you're stuck in a moment you can't get out of'. The key question to ask is if one is open to learning (progressing) or instead stuck in the rut of leaning / dependency (regressing)?

Lear has a fool (court jester), a comedian who accompanies him throughout his life, in the good and bad times. The fool entertains, enlightens, and softens the blows for Lear; he sugarcoats the bitter truth so it becomes palatable and digestible. Like a loyal friend, this court jester is able to feed Lear's mind with the right medicine, and thereby painlessly awaken his conscience to the truth.

When that shock comes to you, and you realize that you've made a *fool* of yourself, you go *deep into introspection* and reflect on the spectrum of vices and virtues within.

How do we interpret this today? Basically, genuine self-reflection allows for a clear inner vision and recognition of one's negative patterns which in turn will help to kill old negative patterns. Ruby Wax, an American comedienne based in England, said the only way to keep the negative at bay is to have faithful guard dogs within your mind, to snarl and eat away at any and all traces of negativity which emerge in the mind before they manifest in your daily life.

CHILDREN OF HATE

Leonard Cohen aptly describes the act of lovemaking and procreation as 'new skin for old ceremony'. Then again, in the consciousness of the Iron Age, every procreation is also through the consciousness of lust. To understand this, one must be clearly aware that there is no being today who is procreated by two humans bringing body, heart, mind, and soul coming in as one to procreate a human being through the consciousness of true love. So it's lust driven—our limited understanding of pure love, because we are all currently 'under the influence' and coloured by the Iron Age we live in.

In extreme cases, such as in a world of war, it is worse where children are procreated through a process of hate. *Newsweek* magazine ('Born Under A Bad Sign', September 22, 1996) covered the Bosnian war, in which, 'It is estimated that 50,000 women were raped. No one knows how many children were born from those rapes. Most pregnancies ended in abortions rather than births. But some women were too far along for an abortion by the time they reached a doctor. Hardly anyone is willing to talk about the babies they had—"children of hate", they are sometimes called.'

When soldiers rape women specifically to impregnate them to perpetuate their misguided creed, it results in children of hate, even if the child should bear no guilt in the equation and deserves only love.

Then we wonder why people get misguided, because if one is a procreation of lust anyway, one is not going to be as fulfilled as a person who is procreated through unconditional love. Consequently, you're naturally (as in 'human nature') going to be driven by the vices. It is therefore going to be more difficult for you to engage with your spiritual side and virtues.

So, if you make a constant effort to stay within your realm of being driven by virtues, in time, it becomes effortless. It's natural being true to the self, which generates a positive charge whenever you interact with another.

You're actually mastering time and you're becoming a self-sovereign. You're taking back your kingship; you're taking back your self-respect, your self-esteem. But when you get upset, you actually are de-throning yourself from the seat of self-respect, giving a chance for the vices to usurp your seat of power, and thereby attracting and experiencing negativity.

When one looks deeper in the knowledge, there are three master drivers. The first is when you are driven by others (*Parmat*). The second is when you are driven by yourself (Ego) (*Manmat*). The third is when you are driven by the divine qualities that you were born with (*Shrimat*). Being driven by the divine will always keep you virtuous. *Parmat* means you're depending too much on others driving you. *Manmat* is being driven by your own mind and your own ego, and *Shrimat* is basically being driven by your inner truth, original values, and remaining truthful at all times.

According to Anthony Strano, 'A love-filled relationship is the deepest desire of the human soul.' It is said that men fall in love (through their eyes) with the woman they are attracted to, and women are attracted to the person they fall in love with (through their ears). That is to do with feeling and the transition and evolution from the shallow physical to encompass deep spiritual feelings. Becoming a holistic being. Living life in all it's glory. So when a man is attracted physically, and the attraction is genuine, it will open up the doorways of the heart, mind and soul. The result can be an intense release and opening of the heart chakra which can be experienced as a gushing waterfall the size of Niagara falls - all within the confines of your heart. The first "S" of S.A.R.A.H.S. represents the physical (S.ex), and we go through the spectrum of letters to the last "S" which represents the S.piritual (love). So, a 'soul mate' is simply one who is able to communicate with another's conscience. It is being true to the conscience, which is the heartbeat of the soul. In that heartbeat, if you put that heartbeat to sleep, then it's easy to be untrue to yourself.

> *'Men learn to love the person that they're attracted to, and women become more and more attracted to the person that they love.'*
>
> SEX, LIES, AND VIDEOTAPE, 1989

If you keep that heart alive, awake, beating constantly, and sensitizing you to the world, being subtle enough to recognize what's going on and being true to your 24-carat self, that golden self within you, you will experience catharsis.

If you're lucky, the cathartic process can be a visualization, a R.E.M. sleep dream, any *mild* shock in your life, and if you stay true and open to knowledge, it can be the *enlightening* tap on your shoulder that says, 'Hey, it's got nothing to do with me but I have to tell you something.' Someone may shock you with the truth and bring you back to enlightenment of the truth, to safeguard you, and raise your level in life. Friedrich Nietzsche's timeless observation states, 'That which does not kill us makes us stronger.'

What is it bringing back? It's finding your true inner compass to drive your external life. Everything happens for a reason, and when you keep a clear awareness of your inner landscape and which terrain you're in, a clear conscience will guide you through.

The negative electricity of the mind is expressed eloquently in 'God Part 2', a song by U2, which was dedicated to John Lennon. With all the negative electricity of the mind in this Iron Age, Bono (the ultimate artist) is able to carve a way out of the darkness by following the light and positive reality of the Love that conquers all negativity and illusion.

It's very simple. The landscape of your mind has everything in it. What choice are you going to make? Because those negative thoughts are going to escape at times and cause inner havoc, releasing the bullets out of the metaphorical Uzi in your hands; and your inner being, when you examine it with your spiritual intellect (the inner microscope), knows very well that there are going to be repercussions. But the external pomp and circum-stance of the company you keep and of the world around you will try to entice you down that road.

There's True North, and there's magnetic North. The deeper question that's being asked in Sting's 'Why Should I Cry For You' is 'Would North be true?' When craving for someone he is deeply in love with, and with feelings he cannot deny or come to terms with, he observes that 'dark angels follow me over a godless sea...

but would North be true?' While the magnetic pull of physical attraction is so powerful, it is only an elevated and enlightened soul who constantly works with that inner compass in search of 'true north'. It's being truthful to yourself, finding your true inner compass to drive your external life accurately.

Abraham Lincoln noted, 'A compass, I learnt when I was surveying… it'll point you True North from where you're standing, but it's got no advice about the swamps and desert and chasm that you'll encounter along the way. If in pursuit of your destination, you plunge ahead, heedless of obstacles, and achieve nothing more than to sink in a swamp, what's the use of knowing True North?' We can all find a map and a compass, but the map is not the journey. In reality, one must learn to metaphysically dance on the heads of snakes in the current world. We have to make the journey for ourselves, and must be alert and ever ready for every consequence.

CHAPTER FIVE

BEWARE OF FALSITY

MACHIAVELLIAN MARKETING

Today, we have many shiny, glittering things distracting us. I have discussed pharmaceuticals. It is the field that made my family prosper. Many years ago, a young executive from Parke-Davis echoed my sentiments that he was proud of being involved in the healthcare industry, as we are involved in 'good karma' by bringing wellness to all. Yet looking back on it holistically, there are a number of negative sides to the industry, such as when profits outweigh concerns for humanity.

Let's consider, for example, the problems caused by the dangerous drug thalidomide, once used against nausea and to alleviate morning sickness in pregnant women in the middle of the last century. These are chemicals that promised something beneficial, but turned out to have devastating side effects.

So let's take a look. You've got everything in front of you. Let's talk about this false notion of medicine which is not the health industry or the wellness industry. Instead, I call the negative part of it 'the sickness industry', promoting lifestyles that allow people to live with their bad habits, which are actually destructive to their health.

With a lot of the big multinational pharmaceutical companies that I have known, I have seen an evolution of products that have been distributed in the name of wellness. However, sometimes these medicines are nothing better than the old bottled snake oil that was a supposed panacea. The chain of snakes can be likened to an anaconda, which unravels its vicious form little by little, and becomes larger than life only to swallow you whole like a boa constrictor.

In 2007, Bristol-Myers Squibb paid more than $510 million to settle charges of illegally marketing and pricing its products, and for alleged bribes to healthcare providers. In 2008, Merck & Co. were fined more than $650 million over failure to pay healthcare rebates for the cholesterol drug Zocor and pain reliever Vioxx. Another company, Cephalon, agreed to pay $425 million to settle allegations that it marketed three drugs for non-approved uses. In 2009, Eli Lilly & Company paid $1.4 billion to settle probes into sales of Zyprexa, a schizophrenia drug, for unapproved uses. The same year, Pfizer pleaded guilty to criminal charges relating to promotion of the now-withdrawn Bextra pain medicine and 13 other drugs, and agreed to pay $2.3 billion. The seven whis-tle-blowers in the company received an approximate payout of $102 million. In July 2012, GlaxoSmithKline paid $3 billion for illegally promoting the anti-depressants Wellbutrin and Paxil, and for failing to disclose safety data about the diabetes drug Avandia. One may question is if this 'Healthcare' or rather 'Hell-th-care'?

There was a time when Freud claimed that cocaine was going to be a panacea. It was a common drug of the time. Remember that until 1907, Coca-Cola contained traces of cocaine, hence its name. It's now known that cocaine is highly addictive. The first batch of Coca-Cola was brewed in 1886 by John Stith Pemberton, a pharmacist, who described the product as a 'brain tonic and intellectual beverage'.

Pharmaceutical companies conduct a lot of marketing. You have steroid preparations that are used and misused, sold in makeshift cosmetic shops in Africa as skin bleachers; mercury-based soaps that were used to literally 'burn' black skin, to lighten it. Skin lighteners today still exist, common in South Asia and Africa, misused in a massive way. In India today, many companies use celebrities as 'brand ambassadors', claiming fairer skin is a guarantee of success, continuing a taboo against dark skin.

The approach is almost Machiavellian: As long as a result is coming through, many products can continue to be used, as well as misused. Some of those key products aimed at correcting the menstrual cycle of women often make it more regular. However, very often, they are contraindicated in pregnancy and thus many have become misused as abortion pills. So a product takes off like wildfire once it's known to be something that can work in aborting a child. At the end of the day, pharmaceutical companies turn a blind eye, as long as results are coming through. In time, the World Health Organization 'finds out', and abruptly bans the product. However, there's always another product waiting around the corner to be misused and abused.

THE SICKNESS INDUSTRY

We have many examples of such products within this industry. For instance, in treating dyslipidemia (abnormal amount of lipids, e.g. cholesterol and or/fat, in the blood,) a disorder of lipoprotein metabolism, statins have been used rampantly to tackle cholesterol. However, current research reported in the media state that there is a possibility that regular use of statins increases your chances by 30 per cent of getting diabetes. Diabetes, again, is said to be the mother of all sicknesses, which also leads to erectile dysfunction, among many other problems. Not something most men would choose to have!

Basically, it ends up being a jackpot for companies to produce those lifestyle drugs, which users are then dependent on for their entire lifespan. The Chief Medical Officer in the UK recently (2013) said that Pharma companies (in their greed for increased revenue and profits) have increasingly opted for producing 'lifestyle drugs', instead of creating new antibiotics, resulting in a dangerous lack of the latter. She further noted that this is causing problems in the pharmaceutical industry that are potentially worse than terrorism, in terms of the general risk to the population. What she meant was that no new antibiotics have been formulated since 1984. If the emergence of new 'super bugs' create new mutations of infections which are resistant to all our current antibiotics, then we will all have hell to pay.

Pharmaceutical companies driven by greed of the 'bottom line' are not interested, because one uses antibiotics only for an infection, generally a one-shot deal and that is the end of it, at least until the next infection. Yet, lifestyle drugs can be used every day. If it's something for dyslipidemia, you can be on it for life; the same with the drugs for tackling diabetes. In the case of erectile dysfunction, surely you're going to use it for a long time, and always at your 'regular' convenience. We have Cialis (Tadalafil), which the industry has nicknamed 'le weekender', because within the current life and work scenario, one works 'like a dog' from Monday to Friday, and on Friday one 'pops that pill' and the effects will last for 36 hours, to 'party' all weekend, and the erectile-enhancing effects 'taper off' just about in time to have lunch with the kids on Sunday. Invariably, these drugs that are being produced also fuel vices, because they are saying, 'Stay in hell, or continue your unwarranted, excessive lifestyle, because we have some magic bullets for you that will tackle it.'

Canderel (Aspartame), for example, we knew early on causes nervousness and memory loss, and excessive use could cause one to become violent. From the horse's mouth, I heard over 30 years ago, 'Well, it doesn't matter. In 20 years from now when they find out, we will have made our millions'. No scruples.

Many drugs basically sustain the bad habits and vices. As I explained earlier, the conscience never dies. It just goes to sleep. What you can do is keep it intoxicated well enough to ensure it stays asleep, so you can continue being driven by the vices. The 'heartbeat' is fast asleep, and unable to alert you, warn you, or let you feel the truth within. The more you're driven in that way, the more it destroys the rest of your body, and also your life. The ultimate balance of six main facets, i.e. body, mind, spirit, family, friends, and business, is lost.

As I mentioned before, if you don't look after your body, you'll end up in hospital. If you don't look after your mind, you could end up in a mental asylum. If you don't look after your spirit, your life can be experienced as a living hell. Then you have your family, your friends, and finally your business, or career. If anything is imbalanced, it will manifest itself. For example, if someone says I'll give you a billion dollars, it would make you very happy, until the same person puts in a condition—and that is that you will have to sacrifice at least one of your eyes. It certainly would create a massive imbalance in your life. A good friend of mine always reminds me 'there's no such thing as a free lunch', his way of encouraging me to exercise, be fair in life, and not take anything for granted. Nothing is ever for nothing.

And what of the side effects? The psychotropic drugs now are being mixed with erectile dysfunction drugs. There's a lot of mess worldwide, so I'm not pointing only at the multinationals, but I'm also pointing at some manufacturers around the world that are not properly regulated, having the freedom to manufacture drugs, combining them, so you have sildenafil, better known as Viagra, mixed with fluoxetine, better known as Prozac. Rest assured that it's a surefire cocktail to keep one deep in the realm of falsehood.

Viagra was originally promoted to 'put love back into relation-ships', but in fact, as long as these erectile dysfunction drugs are misused and abused worldwide, it keeps the machinery going. Whether it's child abuse, whether it's any form of abuse, pros-titution, rape, or war crimes perpetuating 'children of hate', it's happening. A Filipino woman interviewed by *Time* magazine at the time when Viagra was launched remarked, 'Don't the fools know that the number one sex organ is not the one between the legs, but rather the one between the ears?' So again, we've taken the mind out of what we do.

It changes the whole system, the whole world order into the negative. We had problems, like dewormers for instance, which are now banned. Earlier, the brand Antepar (piperazine) was promoted as a dewormer which worked by destroying the nervous system of worms, so one could use a purgative and easily expel the worm. They later found that it was also weakening the nervous system of human beings. Gradually, the product was banned and phased out, but it is still being used in the third world, and the raw material is still available freely. That was actually marketed originally by Wellcome Foundation which, through its various mutations in the past 30 years, is now the high and mighty GSK, currently the largest pharmaceutical corporation in the world.

What CEOs need to do is go on a pilgrimage to the landscape of their brilliant minds, and search for the light and what are right 'pills for a grim age', the right 'pills to clear up a grim image'. Not to concern themselves about demanding their rights, but rather doing what is right. Whenever you earn on the basis of a win-lose paradigm, a payback within the karmic debt cycle is inevitable.

ORGANIZATIONS HAVE A RESPONSIBILITY TO DEVELOP A HOLISTIC CONSCIOUSNESS, A CONSCIENCE WHICH IS WIDE AWAKE, AND REMAIN FOCUSED WITH A BALANCE OF (1) STRONG WILLPOWER, (2) ACCURATE LOGIC, AND (3) A CLEAR UNDERSTANDING WITH MORAL MOTIVES DRIVING THEIR ACTIONS.

Individually, organizations have a responsibility to develop a holistic consciousness, a conscience which is wide awake, and remain focused with a balance of (1) strong willpower, (2) accurate logic, and (3) a clear understanding with moral motives driving their actions. Follow the path of righteousness, and destroy any and all sentiments which are immoral. Ambitions must only be ethically driven, as otherwise one will have no option but to 'bow the head, and wait for the ricochet', as Deep Purple's enlightened 'Child in Time' knows only too well.

JOHN DELOREAN AND FALSE DREAMS

Let's leave the realm of drugs and enter that of cars. The story of John DeLorean is a power-packed microcosm of learning for all those in executive positions in organizations worldwide. It is a prime example of a man who is undone, at the crucial moment, by his own greed. It reminds us why it is so important to remain within, reflecting with humility on the inner landscape of the mind, and never to be driven by one's ego caught up in the outer world with its 'sinking sand trap' into oblivion. To quote Kahlil Gibran:, 'For what are your possessions but things you keep and guard for fear you may need them tomorrow? And tomorrow, what shall tomorrow bring to the over prudent dog burying bones in the trackless sand as he follows the pilgrims to the holy city?'

John DeLorean is a prime example of a man who is undone, at the crucial moment, by his own greed.

For corporate titans, the ultimate bling is not expensive jewelry or a private jet. It's the some remarkable memorable icon that can define a life's achievement. Steve Jobs satiated the world with his the once-bitten Apple; Ray Kroc proved his Midas touch by making the world follow him through the Golden Arches of "M"cDdonald's; Renée Lacoste immortalised his legacy with a miniature green crocodile on quality clothing, making it a premium lifestyle brand for all seasons and ages; Walt Disney's Princess Castle achieved his original aim of keeping his children entertained, and in turn opened the gates of this castle for the child in all of us.

Hillel Levin, in his book *John DeLorean—The Maverick Mogul* (1983) charts the rise and fall of a man who could so easily have been one of the great automotive innovators of the late 20th century. Although John DeLorean was not nearly as successful as any of those the above-mentioned great paradigm shifters, he did have an icon, his namesake car. Thanks to the publicity that saturated its debut in 1976 and the starring leading role in the *Back to the Future* movies which starred Michael J. Fox, the DeLorean with its sleek stainless steel body and gull wing mid doors remains one of the most recognizable cars ever to come off an assembly line.

The car's signature style was a master stroke, but failure to pay attention to detail proved his DeLorean's downfall, hurtling him from the heights of jet-set celebrity into corporate bankruptcy and a notorious cocaine bust, two criminal trials and a host of civil suits that hounded him until his death in 2005.

It is also a cautionary tale about a founding CEO who focused so intently on his company's gleaming image that he became blind to the substance behind it.

What went wrong?

As Levin observes: 'His patents for transmission and suspension systems were noted by GM executives, who plucked him from the dying Packard Motor Company to make him director of advanced engineering for Pontiac' *(Levin, 1983)*. While at Pontiac, he developed a line of so-called 'muscle cars' before moving from engineering into marketing.

There he proved equally adept, cannily exploiting the lucrative synergy of contemporary pop-music, beautiful people and fast cars.

In 1973, he left GM rather suddenly. It subsequently transpired that he had an undeclared ownership stake in a video system, and this system, thus Levin, had been forced on Chevy dealers *(Levin, 1983)*.

This was to be the first of many dubious deals made by DeLorean, yet for many, he was still bathed in the aura of success, bolstered by his playboy lifestyle, his charisma and his glamorous wives.

As if to match the gleaming exterior of the DeLorean, he did some work on his own image—shedding fat, adding muscle, and altering his face with cosmetic surgery. His embrace of youth culture would be complete when he left his first wife to marry a 19-year-old by the name of Kelly Harmon. He was 44 at that time, more than old enough to be her father.

When he made it known that he wanted to start his own car company to produce a so-called 'ethical car,' the DeLorean DMC 12 with its iconic gull wing doors and shiny steel bodywork, a car intended to be fuel-efficient, durable and safe, he had no shortage of financial backers.

He cherry-picked the brightest engineers and mixed them with celebrities like Sammy Davis Jr. and Johnny Carson to fund his project. He even secured a controversial $100 million from the British Government to build the factory in wartorn Belfast in Northern Ireland. It could be said that the Labour Government of the time did not conduct its due-diligence thoroughly enough. They were also blindsided by the gleaming DeLorean.

At this stage, things could still have worked out for DeLorean, despite the various blots that had accumulated in his ethical book. However, there were myriad technical problems with the model and DeLorean ignored the siren calls of his engineers who were desperate for more time. When DeLorean's chief engineer complained, he was shocked that the company's founder was not interested. 'John', he later told a reporter, 'just didn't have time for the details'. The idiom 'the devil is in the detail' derives from the earlier phrase, 'God is in the detail', expressing the idea that whatever one does should be done thoroughly in a higher consciousness. It is a fact that without proper *attention*, one *invites tension*.

The resulting cars were a disaster. Among other things, they had problems with suspension, with alternators that burned out and with an underpowered engine. However, DeLorean seemed unperturbed. He continued to pursue his jet set lifestyle. DeLorean used a sham vendor with no more than a Swiss mailbox to purloin $14 million in British funds. Indeed, making money, not making cars, seemed to occupy DeLorean's attention from the moment he secured British funding.

But as more and more people realized that the car was a dud and dealers were unable to sell them, unsold vehicles started backing up like plague of rats. Nature rebelling—similar to a pathetic fallacy manifesting itself. Clearly, DeLorean had a big 'rat' in his 'strategy' for life. Even the most unsophisticated worker realized that the DeLorean bubble had burst. It took several more months for the company to fall into receivership and the British took possession of the factory.

Even at this stage, DeLorean could have retained some vestige of entrepreneurial credibility. Instead, he tried to raise funds selling his inventory to a pair of slick liquidation experts.

This ill-advised deal, which he barely read before signing, put him into an inextricable financial chokehold. Drowning in debt, with the collective snakes of ego, lust, anger, greed and negative attachment tightening their stranglehold around his throat; these demons in his mind knocked him unconscious, his conscience fast asleep. This opened the doorway of his mind into illusion, making him believe that the angel at the end of his dark tunnel was a dodgy neighbour of his Southern California avocado ranch. In return for stock in his virtually worthless shell company, the perceived 'saviour' was willing to give DeLorean a $10 million share of cocaine smuggled in from Colombia.

On the afternoon of October 19, 1982, when DeLorean arrived at the Los Angeles hotel to pick up his money, the goods were trotted out for him to display. He grabbed a kilo from the pile, held it aloft, and proclaimed it was this is as 'good as gold'.

It turned out to be a sting by the Feds. With his conscience fast asleep, he fraudulently almost reached 100 on the game of snakes and ladders, until he was bitten by the largest snake of all and came crashing back to zero. Bitterly refusing to accept the truth, he resorted to using his lawyers to fight to his way out of this predicament, which included several counts of fraud and racketeering for the $14 million he had stolen from the British government with Colin Chapman, his partner and founder of Lotus Cars. Chapman had already died of a heart attack shortly after the DeLorean drug bust.

Delorean pleaded entrapment, and escaped with an acquittal. However, his reputation was irrevocably destroyed. The coke bust made into DeLorean into a notorious clown in the eyes of the world.

In the UK, he was convicted *in absentia* but of in similar charges along with Chapman, and Chapman's partners in Lotus cars. Although the U.S. Government couldn't imprison DeLorean, it did trash his name. Creditors carved up his assets. No one would hack away more than one of DeLorean's former lawyers. He was sued to collect unpaid legal fees in one judgment in excess of $5 million dollars, forcing DeLorean to sell his New Jersey estate and raid his children's trust funds. In the end, DeLorean would not even own the rights to his own life story.

GM executives now looked back on the history of the DeLorean company, amazed at how close it came to success. With a little more attention to detail, DeLorean could have joined the pantheon of path-breaking entrepreneurs. Instead, despite a number of other projects, he died at age 80 in 2005, forever known for his greed-fueled mistakes rather than his ultimate creation.

NO REGRETS

Being immersed in the world, you are open to advise 'bulleting-in' from every angle and walk of life. I always respect and remember good and 'tough' advice.

At one stage in my life (pre-university), I was confused about my path of study and wanted to venture to become a film director (at the time, a formal degree in this career was non-existent) instead of enrolling in a business studies degree. A tough Navy officer careers guidance counsellor advised, 'What you really need is to put nappies on'—his way of locking my mind out of what he considered 'childish' thoughts. So he used his *willpower and logic* in his advice to me. At the same time, an excellent lecturer in English advised me directly from the *'heart of understanding'* to 'do whatever you love, and you'll never regret it'. Great advice. But, I finally turned to one of my favourite lecturers, who sat me in his office, chucked me a can of beer, as is pretty normal in England, and after we said 'cheers', he immediately said, 'Listen, what did I graduate in?' I said, 'Drama, sir.' He then asked, 'And what am I doing?' I said, 'Teaching English.' He said, 'Well, have I made my point? There's a hell of a world out there. Go and do your business studies. After that, you pursue whatever you want.' That was certainly great advice and completely focused with all the three key ingredients of *willpower, logic, and the heart of understanding.* It anchored me to move forward in life. However, in time to come, I also experienced and noted that by the time the realm of being in business eats into you, it is possible to lose that creative side of you. You lose some of those dreams. That's life, really. It's interesting how life evolves according to what one focuses on. Wherever your mind goes, energy flows.

> BY THE TIME THE REALM OF BEING IN
> BUSINESS EATS INTO YOU, IT IS POSSIBLE
> TO LOSE THAT CREATIVE SIDE OF YOU.
> YOU LOSE SOME OF THOSE DREAMS.

ANATOMY OF THE SOUL

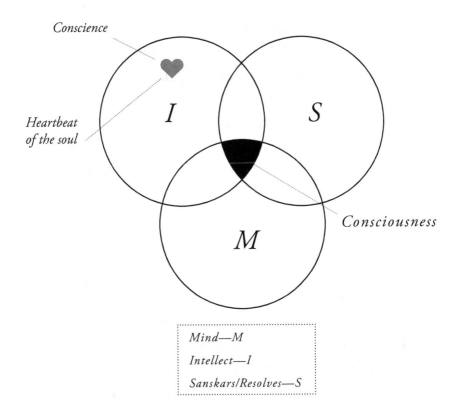

Conscience

Heartbeat
of the soul

I

S

M

Consciousness

Mind—M
Intellect—I
Sanskars/Resolves—S

The anatomy of the soul is never taught. When one is a baby, the parents ask questions to make the baby aware of his body: 'Where's your nose? Where are your eyes? Where are your ears?' But no one really tells you about your 'inner soul', the 'being within' which animates your 'birthday suit' that you came into this world with. The soul has its own M.I.S. (management information systems) in three faculties: (1) the Mind, (2) Intellect, and (3) *Sanskars* (Resolves / The master database of recordings, memories, and past accounts). The mind is the one that rides the five horses, our physical senses. That's where everything happens. The controlling guide for the mind is the Intellect (which houses Faith, and the heartbeat of the soul—the conscience).

The intellect being referred to here is the spiritual intellect, also known as the third eye, which can be likened to a microscope that observes all the activity of the mind, which is connected to our sense organs. Think of when a physically blind man says, 'Oh, I see'; what he means is that he is seeing with the third eye, the inner eye of realization. The *Sanskars* are the database of resolves holding the results of the past baggage that is brought forward each day, and also from past lives. Even in your early life, if you saw a dog biting someone, today you have a fear of dogs because that image and experience has been recorded, and rests in the faculty of Sanskars.

THE INTELLECT BEING REFERRED TO HERE IS THE SPIRITUAL INTELLECT, ALSO KNOWN AS THE THIRD EYE, WHICH CAN BE LIKENED TO A MICROSCOPE THAT OBSERVES ALL THE ACTIVITY OF THE MIND WHICH IS CONNECTED TO OUR SENSE ORGANS.

Unlike Aristotle's *tabula rasa* (blank slate) theory, stating the mind of the individual is born like a 'blank tablet', the faculty of the sanskars ensures that all records of our past experiences are brought forward at birth, and carried forward at physical death to our next birth in the eternal cycle of life. Of course, with the faculties of the mind and the intellect, it must be emphasized that the individual has complete freedom to author his or her own soul. However, the recordings of all past actions in the faculty of the sanskars will exert influence on the level of freedom in actions, circumstances, thoughts, and willpower.

GEMS FROM THE OCEAN OF WISDOM

'As I do so I become. Every action that I perform is recorded in me. These imprints and habits ultimately mould my character and destiny.'

The power of Faith is never brought forward; it is something which is developed in every new life, every rebirth, and rests in the faculty of the intellect. Faith is the ability to see something, even if it's not visible in front of you. The heartbeat of the soul, the conscience or the heartbeat, also rests in the intellect. That is why when people behave in a way which is contrary to reason, faith, and clear conscience, you think, 'How the hell could he do that?'

It's because their conscience was fast asleep. The intellect was in a state of 'blackout'. The microscope (divine eye) is off and is unable to look into what the mind was doing. It's very simple.

PEACE SIGN

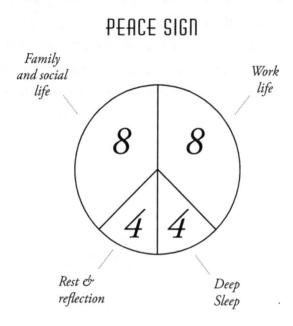

Family and social life

Work life

Rest & reflection

Deep Sleep

The peace sign is split into three divisions of eight hours. But even the lower one is again split. This is symbolic of a life of peace within the 24-hour clock face. Perfect time management. One's life would be in balance and completely fulfilled in all areas of life. One would work diligently for eight hours. Then one would have eight solid hours for family and social interaction. And, finally, eight hours for rest and reflection, which would include four hours of Delta Deep Sleep and four hours of meditative reflection.

The deep delta wave sleep allows the body to restore muscle, tissue, bone, and blood cells that may have been damaged, destroyed, or died off during the course of the day, and releases and/or produces hormones that regulate many of the vital functions of the body. It is the very lack of such quality sleep which weakens the immune system, making our bodies prone to sickness. The four hours of meditative reflection can be likened to REM sleep, which leaves one completely refreshed. REM sleep facilitates creativity by combining certain associative elements into new combinations that are necessary or helpful for problem solving. You're not living half a life in search of squeezing some sweetness, *la dolce vita*, out of a hard-working life, or 'working like a dog', as in the Beatles' song, "A Hard Day's Night", or sleeping like a log—'dead wood'. Imagine if you had eight solid quality hours for family and social life every single day. That would indeed make for a life fulfilled and you would be a very complete person.

Then we have the peaceless sign, which is the sign of the Iron Age today. That is why we talk about wishing we had enough money to do whatever we wanted to do. That is 16 hours of work. One works for eight hours, but invariably takes the 'work' home, and the work experience overlaps into personal life, so in effect, we are all working in a virtual 'sweatshop'.

New York City is a perfect example of a 24-hour lifestyle; hence the mental electricity is buzzing at a high frequency. That work ethic, that drive, has destroyed the peace. When there's peacelessness around you and everyone's a workaholic, you end up being like that. Your environment colours you. Then you get burnt out. There's not enough time left for family and social life. Consequently, we are all too familiar with the kind of problems that result from this lifestyle.

You are coloured by your company. As Mark Twain said, "In Boston they ask, how much does he know? In New York, how much is he worth? In Philadelphia, who were his parents?" Charles Dickens gives a directive in finding a balance in *Hard Times*: "Have a heart that never hardens, a temper that never tires, a touch that never hurts."

What is true balance? Family, friends, and business evenly divided. If you are wise enough to perceive how important true balance is, and how much is enough and really look after that holistically, then you've succeeded.

The most astute poker players in the world know exactly when to either 'hold 'em, or fold 'em'. They remain balanced within while being immersed in the entertaining chaos of the game. When situations in life become like a puzzle, the best advisors have taught me that in a split second it's time to 'cut your losses, and move on'—just put your best foot forward, find direction, correct balance, and move on.

CHAPTER SIX

THE DEEPER IMPACT OF OUR CHOICES

THE DOGS OF WAR

Almost 500 years ago, Niccolò Machiavelli said, 'Wars begin where you will, but do not end where you please.' We've seen his comments still hold true in the modern era, looking currently at both Iraq and Afghanistan, and also the Vietnam war which taught us all the types of lessons one could never learn even in the most prestigious university in the world (even though the death toll was just over two million, compared to the WW2 death toll of sixty million plus).

Still, the true beginning for war is that it starts in the mind. As in the song 'Nineteen' about the Vietnam war by Paul Hardcastle, there's a sample quote from a soldier, namely, Peter Thomas, where he constantly repeats, 'I wasn't really sure what was going on.' Bruce Springsteen's rock anthem, "Born in the USA", is simultaneously caustic, euphoric and cathartic in drumming out the psyche of the Nation that "went out to kill the yellow man".

No one really knows what the hell is going on in the chaotic nightmare of war. That is when everything dies in front of you. Shakespeare's eloquence in *Julius Caesar* provides the phrase, 'Cry havoc and let slip the dogs of war!' Havoc is a military order permitting the seizure of spoil after a victory, and let slip is to release from the leash. The dogs of war are the vices within that you let slip, and then everything in front of you can be destroyed. It was in the *Bhagavad Gita,* on the battlefield of Kurukshetra, where this divine knowledge was imparted to Arjuna, as he was also not 'really sure of what was going on'. For Machiavelli, we know, the 'end justifies the means'; it doesn't matter how you do it, as long as you win. It's certainly not always about that; hence, being Machiavellian is used to denote a villainous mindset.

I would like to share a treasure which was given to me 32 years ago by two of my favourite friends, both American Marines, 'officers and gentlemen' of the highest calibre—from whom I learned the true meaning of *Semper Fi (Semper Fidelis*—Faith Always), and partied with to the sounds of Van Halen, Triumph, and others.

The treasure I refer to is a song by Triumph called 'Fight the Good Fight', which is included in the 'essential tracks' section of this book.

In fighting the fight for good, the game of Snakes and Ladders also comes to mind. It originated in India as an ancient educational game used to teach moral behaviour. The ladders were placed on the squares of virtue, the snakes on the squares of vices. It taught the players that virtuous behaviour would escalate your progression to Nirvana (heaven), but the vices would make the journey difficult, as you would slip down the backs of the snakes representing the vices.

The Yoga of Humanity brings out the original power of the soul, empowering us to 'climb the ladders' and make the right choices. There are various forms of yoga (literally, 'union') which are paths that connect us to the truth. They are Karma (Action) Yoga, *Bhakti* (Devotional) Yoga, and *Jnana* (Knowledge) Yoga. Here, we envelop all of the above and extract what is useful in the form of the yoga of humanity, the yoga of being a truly good human and playing our accurate part in the drama cycle of humanity. The Yoga of Humanity enlightens us on the fundamental knowledge of God, the ultimate truth of creation, birth, death, the result of actions, the eternal nature of the soul, liberation, the purpose and goal of human existence.

We must be clear, however, that if ever we are dis-empowered and weakened, we can slip down the backs of the snakes by making the wrong choices within our mental landscape, and with the subsequent negative vision and drive, one can even become a Hitler. Hitler was ultimately devoured by the snake he created.

> *'Make the lie big, make it simple. Keep saying it, and eventually they will believe it.'*
>
> —ADOLF HITLER

Yet many of us can be inspired to do harm. I'm going to go into something I've called 'Chemist or Alchemist: The Misuse of Drugs in America's Medicated Army'.

When conducting a word-play with the word 'soldier', the soldier is one who is '*sold*' to '*die*'. The '*die*' is cast for the '*soul*'. Casualties of war are like 'casual' relationships, casual ties, nothing more than a 'one-night stand', just collateral damage. When the intoxication of the inner driver of war—'AIDS' of A.ddictions, I.ntoxications, and D.ependencies wears off, the conscience bites within the protagonists of war. It's wrong. Hence, we have that $300 billion psychotropic drug industry. Instead of having 'nuclear' warheads, what we really need is a '*new*', '*clear*' way of thinking to move forward within the realm of our existence, and ensure we defeat *maya* (illusion) and stay close to the truth.

When Iam was scouting Baghdad's dangerous roads, he had the genuine experience of 'walking through the valley of the shadow of death', while acting as bait to lure insurgents into the open so his army unit could kill them. His unit was growing increasingly despondent. The variety of heavy missions, including such actions as protecting Iraqi police hunting down mortars in Baghdad's basements, following orders at nighttime to bring out and collect the enemy's dead, even when some of the bodies were still alive, had exhausted and demoralised him.

A lack of discernment is common. One can echo once again, 'I wasn't really sure what was going on. You don't always know who the bad guys are.' There is escalating violence against just basic human beings, maybe even against children similar to those loved ones waiting for them back home. It is for all these reasons that we find soldiers relying more and more on medications.

Military doctors diagnose depression after very quick sessions. It's because one has to get 'back to business', get armed and move on.

Just 'dish out' the Zoloft, the anti-anxiety drug Sertraline Hcl. Soldiers also fear admitting problems, since the only solution is to pop pills because no one has time to sit down. We have headline-grabbing news on drones, but the real weapons used so stealthily are those medications. The medications are intended not only to help the troops to keep their cool, but also to keep supporting the already-strapped army to preserve its precious resource, which is its soldiers on the front lines. There is a large percentage, up to 30 per cent of troops, who take these pills regularly. It's always antidepressants (to keep them pumped up during the day) and sleeping pills (to 'play dead' when the day is done), apart from the additional use of illegal drugs which also find their way into the system.

These prescriptions today are unremarkable, because generals in history have shown that even George Washington at Valley Forge ordered rum rations to keep the troops fuelled up. Hitler's Nazi *blitzkrieg* (lightning war) into Poland and France was fuelled by an amphetamine known as pervitin, meant to create super soldiers who never needed to sleep. The U.S. Army also extensively used amphetamines during the Vietnam War.

In West Africa (1990–2005), rebel armies drugged children as young as 10 with a mix of cocaine and ephedrine powder to convert them into doped-out killing machines. Basically, they would slit their arm, put the powder in, and wrap some bandage around it so the drug would be absorbed directly into the blood, and keep them 'fired-up' to perform whatever blood-thirsty activities their demonic minds could conjure up.

The etymology or the origin of the word 'assassin' is simply from *hashish*. Hashish-in. People were forced into an addiction of hashish to commit crimes and assassination, so it's like an 'assassin' 'nation'. The word has the word 'sin', which we have established is 'missing the mark'. Because one is so drugged up and doped, there is no discernment power, and thereby one is driven by those vices within. One has totally missed the mark about being truly human.

The rising use of antidepressants in the Army is also reflected in the civilian population. I am using the Army as an example; it's a microcosm of the world at large. A lot of these drugs are used on people as if they were mere guinea pigs; the soldiers are also likened to 'ready and willing' guinea pigs, due to their predicament—in the majority of cases, a quick 'shortcut'/ prescription is handed out without fully evaluating whether they need it.

There's a huge mental and psychological price as a result of the trauma of warfare and of taking these drugs. Doctors claim that up to 70 per cent can bounce back to normalcy after temporary stress. But they never really fully recover. Such ailments begin as mild anxiety, irritability, difficulty sleeping, apathy, pessimism, panic, rage, uncontrollable shaking, or temporary paralysis. And, of course, when the soldiers get home, the PTSD (post-traumatic stress disorder), coupled with the cocktail of drugs, results in dysfunctionality, broken marriages, suicides, and psychiatric breakdowns.

The mental trauma has become so common that the Pentagon (2013) may expand the list of qualifying wounds for a Purple Heart. Imagine giving a Purple Heart to someone who has been suffering from PTSD. Using drugs to cope with traumas has been in debate for many years. There is no magic pill that can erase the violent images, horror, and trauma of war. The quote from Robert Anderson, 'I never sang for my father', is apt to describe the emptiness and wandering in the mental landscape: 'Death ends a life, but does not end a relationship, which carries on in the survivor's mind, toward some resolution it may never find.'

There's no dwelling time. There are newer drugs coming in with fewer side effects, but the imbalance between seeing the price of war and not feeling able to do much about it, contributes to intense fear, helplessness, and horror.

These are the seeds of mental distress. They imprint it and drive you by your inner fear. Inner FEAR (as defined by Anthony Robbins) is a F.alse E.xperience A.ppearing R.eal. So, all those vices that you're driven by, because the experience is not a real experience, are similar to being in a total daze. Like the Jimi Hendrix song, 'Purple Haze'. The chaotic battlefield is indeed a ripe environment for the widespread prescriptions of these medicines.

In the *Bhagavad Gita,* you have these prescriptions or Rx (literally, 'recipes') for living a righteous life being given by God when the mind is in turmoil. But here, in today's world, you have drugs. 'Take this "bullet in" and get on with it.' PTSD isn't fixed by taking pills. It's just numbed. People feel like they're on drugs all the time. Fighting with the inner demons, some have tried to fight the demons themselves and it's a very tough call, when the world around you is crumbling, and there's no one around to guide you through to the light. A lot of people prefer to just give them the shortcut. Some mood elevators can 'do the trick', but then real expertise is required to keep minds elevated and gradually weaned off the medication. The other massive cocktail of drugs that have been used worldwide in a very negative way are Quaaludes, benzodiazepines, such as Ativan, or Roche's Rohypnol, commonly abused to commit the crime of date rape.

A lot of drug companies really don't mind, as long as they can push their Quaaludes or disco biscuits, because the mind craves that experience of ecstasy. This is why we ask if it is 'chemist' or 'alchemist'. Chemists attempt to 'play God' in using chemicals to correct the negative occurrences and imbalances in the human mind. However, it is rather, the one who guides our protagonist, 'AL the Chemist', who is the true 'Alchemist', one who churns our pathways into gold. One 'who shines white light', and enlightens the golden pathway to the sparkling diamond within all of us.

Finally, let's take heed. 'Wars begin where they will, but do not end where you please.' Today our common 'will' is driven by fear. We all have collectively amassed enough arms and ammunition globally to 'incinerate' every single human being (the entire seven billion of us, and counting) 11-13 times over.

Andrew Feinstein, in *The Shadow World—Inside the Global Arms Trade,* gives a harrowing behind-the-scenes tale revealing the billions of dollars which change hands in the deadly collusion that all too often exists among senior politicians, weapons manufacturers, felonious arms dealers, and the military—a situation that compromises security worldwide and undermines the fabric of democracy.

'War', screamed Edwin Starr (1970), and later Bruce Springsteen in a Live cover version, 'What is it good for?' The answer arises from the depth of a clean and clear conscience with a wise and resounding, 'Absolutely nothing!'

HEAVEN CAN WAIT

'If you are looking for Mother Theresa, she doesn't live in Afghanistan.'

—AN ANONYMOUS C.I.A. OFFICIAL, ON THE COUNTRY'S RAMPANT CORRUPTION AND LUCRATIVE BLACK-MARKET DRUG TRADE, 2012

We were in a place called Barge Matal in Afghanistan.

The sun shone down with a vengeance. Benjamin Volence, 'Benny Volence', he's the benevolent one, our Iam, goes through his entire life having awareness of the dichotomy of the false 'pygmy-self', and true 'God-self' which exists in all human beings. When faced with turmoil, he is sometimes drawn to the negative and then rebounds.

Iam wiped the sweat droplets wearily from his forehead with his left arm and gazed upwards from the trench. The blue sky made him feel homesick and a foreboding thought crossed his mind, and undoubtedly all the minds of his fellow comrades in the first battalion. It was both a simple and complicated one: 'When can I finally go back home?' Ironically, Iam did not realize that today was the day he was going home, to his real home, and not his physical home.

Today, his journey in life would be over. He would reach his final destination. Iam looked around the tiny village with only 500 inhabitants and wondered what he was doing there in Barge Matal. Amongst the deluge of questions in his mind for God, he mused about what strange turns and twists God had worked out in his plan for him to be there. 'When will my questions ever be answered?' Iam never envisioned in his wildest dreams he would *realize* the answers, by being inundated in an ocean of answers with his *'real eyes'* wide open.

Iam undid the button of his flap of the large pocket on the breast of his desert combat clothing and pulled out a pocket calendar with a mini pen attached to the side of it. His father had quickly slotted this into his pocket a few minutes before he picked up his small suitcase. His dad's voice echoed through his mind, 'You will need this, Iam. Hope is a rope that swings you through life.'

The scenes from that day remained distinctly vivid to Iam. First, a letter explaining he had been assigned for duty with the 32nd Infantry Regiment in the mountain division of Barge Matal. The next paragraph talked about patriotism and valour, and, finally, the last few lines stated his job assignment would only be for seven days. That was the saving grace and hope embedded in the harsh reality of the letter.

Then it was all about the emotions: his mother and sister sobbing uncontrollably; his father's face grim; and Iam not having any thoughts, his mind and brain numbed. The next few days passed as in a dream. The laughter and lightness that had enveloped him at home had now turned into sorrow and darkness. Then the truth of the entire letter was exposed by a knock on the door. 'It's time to leave.'

The intensity of the entire situation hit hard again. Iam would turn 19 next week. He had already seen one of the fighters lose his life, a few others seriously injured, resulting in amputated limbs. Iam silently prayed. 'Dear God, it would make me so happy if my birthday present would be to be back in the comfort of my living room with my parents, and younger sister. Make it happen, God. Please.' With that, the tears rolled uncontrollably down his cheek.

Tears, not of sorrow, but of acceptance of the fact that he had been chosen for the job and he had to perform his duty to the fullest. Iam's nature is different from many of the comrades in the Army. He has a lot of faith in the Almighty, for the simple reason that he had recognized the true Father. And although, at times, he becomes disheartened, and his faith is tested, he is still a beacon of strength to his comrades who are experiencing deep trauma leading to constant anxiety, feelings of hopelessness, having difficulty sleeping, and continual expressions of pessimism.

Antidepressants (namely Prozac, Zoloft, and Ambien) became the mainstay for a majority of Iam's comrades, yet not for Iam. His experience of the past three months was no different from those of his colleagues: images of shattered bodies, innocent civilians, and wasted lives of women and children of every age imaginable. The sheer umbrella of guilt takes over your entire being. Yet he hung in there. Control over the mind, he had been taught. 'Observe and don't absorb': go deep within the eye of the storm, stay centred, fill the mind with positive, happy thoughts, and then there will be no space for negative thoughts within any chaos.

It was commendable that Iam had the tenacity to stay with the task at hand—similar to Robert De Niro's character in *The Deer Hunter*, from whom he had always drawn inspiration. Understanding one's *Part* (role) accurately after the *Party* is over. The shedding of the clothes (symbolic of becoming 'detached'), the streaking through the streets (the symbol of humility and fearlessness), realizing that one would have to shed a particular awareness (the comfort of Home) in preparation for the journey to the killing fields (the discomfort of another Home). Preparing yourself accurately to play the hero actor according your role, and the stage of life, with its different platforms.

This is life, and constantly understand it's always just 'As Good As It Gets', the very message which is conveyed in the famous film with Jack Nicholson and Helen Hunt. It's only up to us to make it better.

You can only play your own part, write your own script, and the game is to play it as best as you can. For no one can never play another's part, or write another's script, though many do get caught up in this trap of attempting to control others, and suffer the negative repercussions of this behaviour. Keeping true to our original self will ensure we are not caught up in the imitations and limitations of others.

Iam had learned that his sniper rifle was five times heavier than the weight of an ordinary NATO 7.62 mm gun, and had six times the energy. There were a number of reasons why this particular rifle had been chosen to fight against the Taliban: its power, its broad range (almost two and a half kilometers), and its precision.

However, Iam also knew the negative side. That the bullets were heavy, packed with kinetic energy. They could accurately kill the enemy, but the bullet's powerful follow-through could also put innocent civilians in danger. Before Iam had any more time to think about the repercussions of this deadly weapon, he heard a loud noise and instinctively ducked. The stray bullet headed for the centre of his forehead, a bullet from a high-tech weapon that can fire the enemy from 700 meters away and strike even those taking cover behind walls, rocks, and in trenches. This was why time and again he had been warned never to underestimate the knowledge and the tactics of the Taliban.

The enemy's weapons were superior calibre, a rifle that used a computer chip-embedded round that could detonate behind walls and, in this case, trenches. There was no escape. Iam feels the bullet touch the skin of his forehead. He knows that he has nowhere to run, nowhere to hide. However, Iam's eyes have a clear focus in the situation. He recalls the Creed track 'Hide' from the deep recesses of his soul, and it reverberates within,

> *'To what do I owe this gift my friend? My life, my love, my soul? I've been dancing with the devil way too long, (living with the vices, in a vice-filled world.)'*
>
> —CREED, 'HIDE'

At that split second, he gains full awareness and deep insight. His subconscious calls out to God. In that moment of craving the truth, in his helmet he has playing a song called 'Blaze of Glory.'

'To be shot down in a blaze of glory.
Take me now, but know the truth.'

—JON BON JOVI, 'BLAZE OF GLORY'

The body experienced an explosion of peace as the bullet entered the skull and into the physical brain so that all the organs are disconnected. The body slumps to the ground in slow motion, sending a cloud of dust, which rises into the air, covering the sun's rays and creating a 10,000 mile long, 100 miles wide *path of totality'* eclipse, similar to the one created when the track of the moon's dark inner shadow casts itself across the earth.

Simultaneously, all the militants, enemies included, drop their physical weaponry and shift their gaze upwards as the eclipse accelerates and brings physical darkness upon them. As they forget all their differences, they become increasingly enlightened. The sun's duty is to give light and to destroy all negativity. In this case, the eclipse of the sun, coupled with the events, cleanses negativity.

There is no sign of any physical injury as they see a perfect and pure body, the face of perfect peace, with a small, round dot in the middle of the forehead where the bullet had entered the body. And a realization strikes all those who are present that the dead body lying on the ground is somehow related to the events of nature. The darkness encompasses everyone around and the bodies dissolve into the darkness. Only some points of light remain. Now that the costume of this actor has been shed, the soul, or the point of life, at that split second has to leave the body. It is saturated with high-octane light fuel, faster than the speed of a bullet, the speed of sound, or even the speed of light. The soul is transported

into another realm, another consciousness, a state which psycho-
therapists would refer to as a trance hypnotic regression, accessing
the memories from past lives. In that one second, he is able to
metaphysically relive all the births of his various lives.

Heaven can wait, and perhaps our time is not here. God himself
is prompted into realizing that this is a very special soul and that
he is not to suffer. And because 'anything can be achieved with
the power of prayer, except that which is beyond the will of God'.
What exactly is it that is beyond the will of God? It is the realm of
our actions performed, the parts we play according to our free-will
on the drama stage of life. Our personal karmic accountability.
We already have that original natural law of karma stored in the
database of our psyche: 'As you sow, so you reap'.

Iam had the intuition that the use of unnatural products can
deter him from knowing himself as he truly is. He stayed true to
his original nature, being careful never to be trapped in acquired
negativities of the current world. Of course, he loved rock music,
and once asked someone enlightened why some music reached
the core of truth, and expressed it so eloquently that it made his
soul soar. The answer was simple, that a 'chemical high' can take
you to the truth within, but can never keep you there, hence the
reason for addiction, and subsequent untimely death. One has to
reach the truth and experience super-sensual joy, a joy beyond the
senses, without ever using manmade chemicals. A very spiritual
being, who had in his youth experimented with LSD, explained
the 'high' as a phenomenon in which every pore in his body experienced 'orgasm', but also explained that the feeling was transient
with its negative side effects. Iam was the chosen one because he
makes so much effort within to remain true to himself.

Even if you put yourself into a cage, into any cage in this lifetime, whether physical (handcuffs / jail) or metaphysical (mental trauma), you can come out of it through the *honesty of your heart*. An open and honest heart always attracts God himself to intervene. That soul flies out at rocket speed even before the bullet pierces the head. That's why there's no physical blood or the gushing of blood. That's the point. In Hinduism, the tilak is used to represent the soul. If you ever visit an Indian temple and they apply a red dot (of vermillion powder) to the middle of your forehead, it's to recognize your imperishable self and to indicate that the seat of the soul is housed in the middle of the forehead, just behind the eyes.

> *"When you love you should not say, 'God is in my heart,' but rather, 'I am in the heart of God'."*
>
> —KHALIL GIBRAN

THE WOMB CAN BE A PRISON

Unlike U2's song which claims, 'I still haven't found what I'm looking for', I can claim with conviction that I have found what I am looking for, that inner compass to drive my outer life. It doesn't matter who I come into contact with. As long as I give love and respect to them, they'll always share their truth. Iam also has that kind of philosophy as a soldier.

According to your actions, there is a golden age. We can refer to it as the Age of Paradise when the womb is likened to a palace. You can go to sleep for nine months and be fed and looked after. One can experience such bliss in meditation, and it is sometimes referred to as the 'seed stage'. However, in the Iron Age, the womb is likened to a prison. It's when the soul enters the foetus; the child is then able to experience so much. It experiences that prison, and in that prison it makes a lot of promises with regard to settlement of its built-up of karmic debt. However, when a child is born, Shakespeare's immortal words are apt to describe the moment, 'When we are born, we cry that we have come to this great stage of fools.' Invariably, we then revert to our acquired self.

Every child is born with an accountability of his or her past karmic accounts. Louise Hay, in *You Can Heal Yourself*, also explains that every child chooses the parents and family he or she is born to. To explain this further, when you study *The Prophet* by Khalil Gibran, it starts on a hillside where he ponders, 'If this is my day of harvest, in what fields have I sowed the seed, and in what unremembered seasons?' That's when everyone comes to him for his special sharing about the underlying truth of every facet of life as we know it. He knows his *ship* is coming in, meaning he's about to leave his body. He is a man who is fully enlightened, and lives life in the realm beyond the 'valley of the shadow of death'.

That's why, before he leaves, he is the respected 'wisdom keeper', and the townsfolk all gather and request, 'Prophet of God... now your ship has come, and you must needs go, yet this we ask ere you leave us, that you speak to us and give us of your truth. And we will give it unto our children, and they unto their children, and it shall not perish. Tell us all that has been shown you of that which is between birth and death. Everything shared by him is the "universal truth" coded within all of us.' But Khalil Gibran clothed all those truths with his own poetic style, and was able to reach a global audience with his universal truths. 'A voice cannot carry the tongue and the lips that give it wings. Alone must it seek the ether. And alone and without his nest shall the eagle fly across the sun.' Whether it's about children, marriage, or business, everything is shared as an imperishable universal truth. At the end, he bids a timely 'farewell' to all, stating that though he dies, 'Forget not that I shall come back to you... we (will once again) come together and together stretch our hands unto the giver' (in respect of the Supreme Being).

With reincarnation, this is moving away from the view of life as an absurd (or meaningless) drama and of existential thought which perceives life on a 'linear' plane, with only birth and death as the major events in our lives, and the vacuum in between simply as 'games people play'. With reincarnation, life is a cycle, an eternal cycle of life, death, life everlasting. We have this cycle and, yes, the womb also plays differing roles in the cycles of life. It can behave as a palace in an age that was perfect, where the mental landscape was pure 24-carat gold. But when the cycle of life turns into the Iron Age, the womb can become like a prison.

One way or the other, everything is interconnected. All of our actions are interconnected. We cannot go and earn those millions and be blind about which banker we're with. It really doesn't matter to them. But all of this comes back to us, in terms of our personal accountability. As in the case of Judas, it's simple. His conscience bit him and there was only one way out, as he saw it with his limited perception. He had to commit suicide. He had to 'kill his body', even though he could have chosen to transform himself, to kill his vices within with a higher consciousness, and be 'born again' to continue the work of Jesus's teachings.

To explain the phenomenon of 'blood money', there is a phrase in Hindi which states, 'If you ripped it off aggressively, it becomes blood in your hand, that money. If you ask for it or beg for it or plead for it, it's simply like drinking water. But if it comes through with your good actions, it comes to you like milk. That milk will sustain you, your families, and future generations in the cycle of life and the cycle of time forever.'

The global impact of our decisions is more than simply environmental. It is spiritual, for ourselves and for those around us. This impacts how we work in business.

It is an ocean of opportunity, an endless mushrooming cloud of business. The biggest CEOs in the world will tell you that the way forward today is 'the power of partnerships'. But who are you partnering with worldwide? It is a spider's web with underworld connections. Worldwide banks, third world finance aid, counterfeit currency, and investment in arms and ammunition.

The illegal sales of arms and ammunition is also something I studied as the *marketing of unmentionables* 35 years ago for my marketing thesis. At that time, you couldn't say the word condom without raising a childish snicker or an awe-struck face in the room. London Rubber Co. (originators of Durex) coined the phrase and brand 'Lifestyles' condoms, to make it easier for condoms to be socially acceptable. It was all hush-hush. Of course, now with the advent of AIDS, condoms are promoted openly to safeguard life.

THE FRANKENPHARMACY

The Citizens Commission on Human Rights (CCHR), in a report published by Kelly Patricia O'Meara on October 30, 2012, 'Two

Soldiers Prescribed 54 Drugs: Military Mental Health "Treatment" Becomes Frankenpharmacy', highlighted that the problem of poor mental health care in the U.S. military is actually catastrophic. The devastating adverse effects mind-altering psychiatric drugs may be having on the nation's military troops are best summed up by Mary Shelley. In her novel, Frankenstein, she wrote, 'Nothing is so painful to the human mind as a great and sudden change.' The monstrous psycho-pharmacological experiment is viewed by O'Meara as being largely responsible for the nation's military troops taking their lives in record numbers, while more and more seemingly healthy soldiers are dying from apparently sudden unexplained senseless deaths, ending their tormented lives, and leaving behind grief-stricken families.

At times, it seems that the dark side of the pharmaceutical industry is no better than an illegal drug dealer on the streets. I am reminded of the 2Pac song 'Changes', where he craves to 'Take the evil out the people, (so) they'll be acting right', and then advises a dealer who states, *'I made a G today,'* and tells them, *'But you made it in a sleazy way. Sellin' crack to the kids'.* The reply is forlorn from someone who is caught in a dog-eat-dog rut of life and he simply replies, *'I gotta get paid',* completely blind to what he is doing.

Why is it that the politicians don't do something about regulating this crazy Internet or World Wide Web of deceit, where scenes of graphic and violent sex are being consumed on a daily basis by teenagers, who are then replicating these things in their lives? When those on the seat of power, sitting in their glass houses like all of us, choke their conscience and turn a blind eye on correcting something which is clearly wrong in society, we all will have to face repercussions. Little do you realize that you have to bow your head and wait for the ricochet, like a 'blind man shooting at the world, bullets flying. If you've been bad, and you know you have, simply bow your head and wait for the ricochet'.

"Those who have the privilege to know have the duty to act."

—ALBERT EINSTEIN

You have an ego. It's an anaesthetic. You think, 'Oh, I did good. I supported this and I supported that.' What did you really support? The CEOs are driven, almost like Scarface. When Scarface says, 'You're not hungry anymore. You're not hungry. What are you hungry for?' It's a big blast-out at the end. They just carry on, escalating, because of that greed drive, in which the well is overfilled and is overflowing and still your throat is parched and you can't understand why. Because you don't take time to drink out of that well and find contentment. Take time to drink out of that well of knowledge, and find contentment. Drink from the 'wishing well', and become a 'well-wisher'.

SNAKES IN A CAPSULE

The snakes in a capsule represent a deal with Faust. Every decision that's executed is Machiavellian, only results driven. It doesn't matter who dies in the process. Pfizer released a drug for which they were fined about $2.5 billion by the FDA. The whistleblowers within the company, 10 of them, received a payout of $102 million. It was all in an article unravelling the truth of revenge, betrayal, and power in one of the world's largest drug companies.

THE WHISTLEBLOWERS WITHIN THE COMPANY, 10 OF THEM, RECEIVED A PAYOUT OF $102 MILLION.

The deal with Faust has the implication of 'dust to dust, ashes to ashes' in it. Transient gain, for long term suffering. That's basically what happens when you make a deal with Faust, or the Devil, or the vices within you. This is basically when one is vice-driven. It doesn't have any blessing within it. The snake, the mire, the farm story is a wonderful story.

I had met an American who came into our pharmacy (almost 40 years ago) to purchase some antibiotics, and some anti-snake venom serum, as he was suffering from a 'mild' snakebite. We were very concerned. He 'kindly' invited us to visit his snake farm. It was the first time I'd ever seen someone literally playing with snakes, crawling around him. It called to mind for me the Indian deity Shiva with a snake around his neck.

I myself had an intense fear of snakes from an early age, until I wan enlightened by this 'modern day' snake charmer, Carl. Carl was very kind to the snakes, but in order to conduct his business, he would get snakes angry, almost like Iago invoking that angry 'green-eyed monster' in Othello. When the snakes reacted by attacking with their fangs protruding, Carl would navigate their anger and immediately have them bite the edge of a glass vessel, simultaneously pressing the nape of the snake's neck, squeezing out and collecting their venom. Masterful indeed. He would then freeze the venom, and ship it to the United States, where it would be used to produce pharmaceuticals aimed at treatments (depending on the type of venom), from controlling blood flow in hypertension to treating thrombosis patients. To simplify the complicated, Carl said, 'Snake venom is just like human saliva, only it's about 100 times as potent'. Most snake venom is indeed fatal for humans. Some cause our blood to coagulate, whereas others thin the blood so that the victim bleeds to death. Both coagulants and thinners have their uses in the pharmaceutical industry, and he made a lot of money from the venom-milking process.

Carl gave us an illustrated book which clearly showed that when a snake is slit open, it is like a human being. It has a heart and a stomach. This was a revelation to me. This thing is similar to a human being. I don't need to fear its outer appearance. That knowledge dispelled the FEAR within me, what Anthony Robbins refers to as F.alse E.xperience A.ppearing R.eal. When I was very young (3 years old) and did something naughty, I was locked up in a room (by my grand-dad playing an alternative role of the wise old Cherokee chief) against the wishes of the other 'soft-hearted' family members. However, I am so thankful for that traumatic experience today. The room happened to have a thick coil of rope in one corner. I was always traumatized, thinking the rope to be a snake. The fear definitely made me realise I had to 'clean up my act', so my grand-dad, the lock on the door, and the rope in the corner created a type of mirage, a positive illusion, the perfect incentive for me to become a better person.

In life experiences, there are many ropes around you. You can hold on to them and—just as it is said that 'hope is a rope'—they swing you through life. Once you recognize it's not a snake, it's just a rope, the inner lens of your mind comes into focus, and you see the reality. Dispelling that fear was a very big thing for me, and whenever fear is dispelled in our lives, it creates a paradigm shift which can indeed be a life-changing experience.

When we have the depiction of Shiva, who is really a symbolic depiction of the qualities of God, he has a snake around his neck and is very comfortable, in a meditative pose. This is a symbol that all of the vices have been tamed, all the snakes are calm, and they are now useful in protecting the self, and will follow the directions of their virtuous master. The snakes become like an 'electric fence' of protection, warding off any trace of negativity which may appear at any time. By remaining virtuous, we truly learn how to dance on the heads of snakes, and succeed in a life that is increasingly uncertain. This is metaphysical, a very different phenomenon from the 'snake charmer' who gets the snake 'drunk' by charming it with the sound of his flute and swaying head movements; and also very different from the snake-pit 'dancers' in Thailand, whose snakes are 'punch drunk' on sleep-inducing drugs, and the deafening drumbeat of extremely loud techno / trance music. One can get exhausted when dancing physically, but one can never experience tiredness while dancing in the mind. This form of mind control is exhilarating, and will always generate great energy.

There have been within the pharmaceutical world major disasters where it is the snakes, the vices, especially that of greed, that take control. Thalidomide was touted as a great painkiller for everyone, including preventing morning sickness in pregnant women. The result? Thousands of severely deformed and disabled babies in the United States, Canada, Europe, Japan, and other countries.

The drug and the aftermath brought the company, Grünenthal, to its knees. But other things can cause such deformities too, we have learned. Within the last 15 to 20 years, it's been understood that even excessive Vitamin A can cause foetal deformities. Knowledge of this created a change in the neonatal drug industry, forcing many companies to withdraw products and carry warnings against use in pregnancy.

As I said, people do things and they keep 'pushing the envelope', and then suddenly, *emergency* strikes, like a pop-up jack-in-the-box, or snake-in-the-box, smack in the face. *Emergency* is like *'Emerge'*, and then *'See'*, causing shock. It's only when they collapse to an all-time low that they are ready to listen. Otherwise, their ears are blocked. In our lives, we have to understand those illusions and play with them and have fun with them, and get the best out of them.

Dance on the heads of snakes. Tame the snakes, and never let the snakes intoxicate you, and then consume you.

CHAPTER SEVEN

ENLIGHTENMENT

I t is said that 'when the pupil is ready, the teacher will appear'. Pupil refers to the 'student' within us all, and also is the same word used for the black holes which let light into the eyes, which don't just help us see, but also signal what's going on in our minds. The eyes are the windows to the soul, and the pupils are the windows to the mind. Changes in pupil size (dilation and constriction of our pupils) reveal many aspects of thought. If I'm stimulated by something new, my pupils will dilate a bit at first, but they'll only stay dilated if I continue to be interested.

The reason doctors and paramedics flash a light in patients' eyes is to check if their brains are working normally. They use the acronym *PERRL:* the pupils should be Equal, Round and Reactive to Light. If a brain is damaged in any way, you won't see PERRL, and the intellect will not be able to imbibe the PEARLS of knowledge.

Some drugs, like alcohol and opioids, cause the pupils to constrict. Others, like amphetamine, cocaine, and LSD, cause them to dilate. Police officers know this and some use it as one way of checking to see if one is 'under the influence'.

Generally, when the pupils dilate, it sends a positive message, and when they constrict, it's a negative one. But exactly what it means depends on the situation, and whether someone has turned on a light into the eyes with the aim of setting the consciousness ablaze with enlightenment.

> 'We can easily forgive a child who is afraid of the dark;
> The real tragedy of life is when men are afraid of the light.'
>
> —PLATO

AN ENCOUNTER

'Three square feet' are what we have all been allotted on this earth we call 'home', because within the phenomenon of democracy (literally, power to the people), everybody wants to be a power unto themselves. We all have been allotted three square feet of land on 'lease' (until death do us part) in this world to take a chance to live life to the fullest, and be a walking, talking university unto ourselves. Comparing Khalil Gibran's contrast between the *'God-self'* and *'pygmy-self'* which exist in all of us, today we can either exist in our kindergarten-self, or evolve in the matters of the physical, emotional, mental, and spiritual to a doctorate (PhD) level.

We can maximize our degrees of knowledge and life experience to become a humble authority to share our truth with all in our connection, and serve the world at large. The sharing of truth is the master key that opens our doors to success on the eternal world stage. Worthy leaders will make it their personal mission statement to ensure that before they are 'six feet under, or on that six foot long funeral pyre', that we make the very best use of the three square feet that they have been entrusted with in this lifetime to imbibe the truth, become a walking, talking university, a wisdom keeper, and benefit all those we come into contact with. By sharing the best that life has to offer (to impact positively on others), we will ensure that we find the key to unlock the door to eternal fortune in the cycle of life.

Iam enters another visualization and interaction. We can imagine it as a phone booth, likened to a confession booth that connects Iam to God.

The rain came down with a vengeance. It was almost like a natural karmic payback against the sun for the humidity that had enveloped the Earth's atmosphere in the last few days. Thor, the god of thunder, was at work. The discharge of atmospheric electricity between the clouds created a dangerous flash of lightning that was almost instantly followed by the voluminous roaring, rolling sound of thunder. Ironically, 'lightning' was also slang for the cheap whiskey of poor quality, which is what Iam had been drinking at a street bar that he'd walked into.

He had known that no one would recognize him there and he could drink himself to death without any inhibitions, but as a result, his head thundered from the raw whiskey that he had knocked back within a few minutes. The external storm was almost on a par with the internal storm. Iam's vision was blurry as he drove in his intoxicated state. The wipers of his Mercedes worked overtime, distorting his vision even more.

His head felt heavy and his eyelids closed, despite his will to stay awake. The road was desolate. There were no other cars around. Iam pressed his foot harder on the accelerator and his thoughts were death, the desire to die and to end this life of lies. 'Faith?' questioned Iam. 'What is faith? I have no faith. All I know is that the fate of my life is death. That will answer all my questions. That will give me my peace of mind. That will put an end to my misery. That will wash away this nightmare and all my sins. Yes, suicide is the only answer.'

> *'The dog that is fated to lose its way in the bush will remain deaf to the hunter's whistle.'*
>
> —WOLE SOYINKA

The inevitable happened: the car went straight into a tree. The impact of the fast-moving car against the tree caused the vehicle to overturn.

The blood gushed out of Iam's head and his body shook uncontrollably. He staggered out, stumbled, and saw a telephone booth 33 yards ahead. His mind was at play. There was a purification process going on. Standing in the telephone booth was like standing in a confession booth, or standing upright in a coffin, which can be symbolic of 'dying alive'. Because when you say dying alive, those people who agree to 'die alive' basically agree to confessing and killing their vices and to be driven by their virtues.

All within those three square feet that you have been entrusted with. Your personal three square feet upon which you stand to play your special part on the stage of the world's drama.

'Fallen leaves will always go back to their roots.'

—CHINESE IDIOM

He was scared to enter the booth, his mind a complete mess. Desperate and depressed, craving for somebody to save him, he instinctively dialed out. 3-3-3: the number for God. Within a split second, the phone was answered.

'AL speaking', said a gentle voice.

'Who are you? Where have you come from?' cried Iam. There was a pin-drop silence for a moment, which seemed like an eternity. Silence is the oxygen for the mind, and Iam's mind was receiving this breath of life in preparation for a most unusual reply.

'Who are you? Where have you come from? Those are the most important questions that I need to ask you', AL said softly.

'The best place to start is obviously from the beginning. The song 'Fast Car' has some good advice for you, since you seem to love a Fast Car life, which has "crash-landed" you to this situation at this point in time. It provides the wisdom "starting from zero, you've got nothing to lose".

'AL stands for Alpha, an infinitesimal point of light, the seed, the starting point. Let's rewind time, and go back to the beginning. Another one of my wisdom keepers, Soren Kierkegaard, noted that "life can only be understood backwards, but it must be lived forwards".

'So, let's put a full stop. Reflect, understand, and find that compass to put our best foot forward.'

Iam was forlorn, and almost paralysed, as if in REM sleep.

AL continued, 'My sweet child. It is because of your love for God that you arrived here. I've had to come into your realm of consciousness at this time to accurately introduce myself to you.'

Iam's stone-intellect consciousness was still impervious, despondent, and apprehensive. 'Sweet words' had always 'washed off' him like water off a duck's back, and in life he had only ever used a soft tone with others with the aim of manipulating them. He was now weakened by the accident and by his head wound. He felt almost drained to death.

The phone booth dissolved, and Iam was blinded by white light as AL 'appeared' to him as a shadowed executioner, ready to carve him up. Iam realized that he was going to be sliced apart and the adrenaline began flowing through him like lightning through his veins. His heart and mind pulsated. He felt excruciating pain and he knew this was his conscience biting him inside.

It's similar to the pain Michael Jackson felt, and could never pinpoint, driving him to doctors for a general anaesthetic to facilitate his sleep. Propofol is a short-acting, intravenously administered hypnotic / amnesic agent. On the physical level, it puts the body to sleep. On a spiritual level, it puts the conscience into a deep sleep. Propofol has been referred to as 'milk of amnesia'. Unfortunately for Michael, that sleep became permanent, and the world lost this great talent at the relatively tender age of 50. One can say that MJ was so caught up in making the external world happy that he lacked the milk of human kindness towards himself, unable to tame the inner wolves wreaking havoc in the realm of his conscience—hence, he lived in the realm of falsehood, never being able to experience the true sweetness of a balanced lifestyle.

When Michael Jackson was on trial over alleged child sexual abuse, he paid a $40 million out-of-court settlement. But the pain never left him. Uri Geller (the illusionist and psychic), a good friend of Michael's, stated once that he did something unethical by putting Michael into a trance. It was because he really cared for Michael. Within the trance, he asked, 'Michael, how could you do that to a kid?' MJ's conscience answered, 'How could I ever, ever touch a kid in that way?' Asked about the $40 million payout, MJ replied, while still in the trance of truth, 'I couldn't stand the lies. I couldn't stand it anymore.'

Something had gone astray and the cover-up itself caused a different kind of pain. Of course, years later some of those children did reveal that their parents had told them to lie.

It's similar to the pain that Iam is feeling now, that conscience biting at him. A lot of times when people's conscience bites in settlement of karmic debt, they don't really understand it, and that's when they would rather intoxicate themselves, and basically send a signal to their conscience to 'Play Dead'.

He was feeling that he was going to be executed by the presence of AL, and he had heard that 'cowards die a thousand deaths' before they really die. He waited in that split second to be sym-bolically carved up like an animal in some abattoir. In extremis, he collapsed to his knees when what followed was the kindest voice that he had ever heard. It said 'Iam, I think you're ready for your first lesson. All this negative build-up inside of you, what you're experiencing now is in *"the heart of your soul"*. Your *conscience* is biting you, and chewing you up. Your eyes signal to me that you are ready for the truth.

'It is time, Iam, for you to be kind to yourself. You've completely forgotten the days of your real childhood. This Iron Age has become bankrupt of purity, peace, and happiness, and so you've tortured yourself enough and "enough is enough". The biting of your conscience has brought you to your knees. It is the first symbol that you have been humbled. However, I do not want you on your knees; I want you as my equal, because I created you exactly as I am, in my own image, and cannot stand to see you suffer.

'You're in trouble today because you're skimming the surface of the ocean. You must delve deep in the ocean, live life to the fullest, and leave a legacy; otherwise, all you've had is a "popcorn" existence. The popcorn almost always finishes before the movie is over. The reason why one gets involved in only skimming the surface of the ocean is because one is afraid of what's underneath the ocean, and far too intoxicated with flying on the Jet Skis of life, always in the fast lane.'

GEMS FROM THE OCEAN OF WISDOM

'Life is like a drama. If I understand the plot, there is great happiness.'

'The big problem is that my children are so addicted to suffering that it is difficult to wean them off it. Now that you are ready and you feel it for yourself, you have a listening ear in your conscience. To even commence the lesson, you first have to put your less on. "*Less on.*" Lesson has the word "less", and the switch of "on", which is to do with the realm of your attitude and consciousness. In putting "on" the switch of being "less", you are revealing your humility, and thus openness to learning. In the game of teaching and learning, if you have humility, and respect for the teacher, then the learning is accelerated. Experience is the greatest teacher of all. To understand something, you need knowledge, but to convert it to wisdom, you need experience."

'No matter how dark the situation, one must always hold on to the steady light of hope. The secret of enthusiasm is remarkably simple: live in a state of appreciation. Enthusiasm is a great power. With it, one can never be disheartened, because it simplifies all difficulties. Condition your mind to remain cool under all conditions. This will help you to sow the right seeds of thought. When you build a house, every brick counts; when you build character, every thought counts, so think constructively always. A clean intellect is like the mind's filter separating valuable thoughts from wasteful ones and enabling me to put into action only those of value. Understand: Acceptance is the secret of contentment. Appreciation is the secret of happiness. Contentment is the mother of all virtues."

'I, AL, have affirmed that you will live the life of a carefree emperor using nothing more than the wealth that lives within yourself. It is the seed within each of us which flowers the life which we experience. In order to bring about true transformation, one has to understand the accurate anatomy of the inner seed of existence, the soul. God shows us simply and safely to invest our mind, body, wealth, and time, which we have been wasting on misunderstood personal and collective karmic accounts. The aim is for us to truly achieve physical, emotional, mental, and spiritual independence in life.

'The ultimate spiritual truth is not just to find *mukti* (liberation) by escaping from the world (as Judas did when he committed suicide, thinking that was an escape from his predicament). We can never escape from the eternal world drama, the stage on which we have to play our part. Shakespeare was spot-on when he wrote, "All the world's a stage, and all the men and women merely players: They have their exits and their entrances; and one man in his time plays many parts. His acts being seven ages." However, he refers to the seven ages in one lifetime, but man, in fact, experiences these seven ages over and over again through many lifetimes, and in the different theatres which host the performers. The stages and quality of actors also are apt to the age they enter on stage: Golden, Silver, Copper, Iron, and finally the Diamond stage, before the cycle restarts.'

'Ordinary Man', the song by Triumph, reverberated in Iam's mind: 'Look in the mirror. Tell me what do you see. Or can you lie to yourself like you're lyin' to me? Do you fall asleep real easy, feelin' justified and right, or do you wake up feelin' empty in the middle of the night? You want to think you're different, but you know you never can—You're just another ordinary man.'

In the depth of his darkest depression, he looked into the mirror of his mind and reflected, 'I feel like a prisoner of war. Like I haven't slept for years.' He always felt vulnerable, inadequate, and had always blocked these feelings. For the first time, AL had said something with a fight in it to the man in the mirror, IAM, who had become like a bruised and beaten prisoner of war, MIA— Missing In Action, and losing his AIM in life.

AL whispered, 'Willpower is the first step, and thereafter vision is 100 times more powerful than willpower, and it's the vision which will bring about that exponential change in your fortunes.'

Iam had become a '*beggar*' because he was completely out of synch. Instead of being a bestower of fortune, he was living the miserable stress-packed life of spending tomorrow's 'currency' today. 'I want it now.' The world is in a state of deep illusion, what with quick-fix politicians, almost half of the world's exploding population living below the poverty line, and the media with its twisted reporting. Iam began to see how mixed up he was under the influence of his current realm of existence. He had to find a lifeline to his deadlines in life, and AL would show him the way, enlighten his path. He realized that he would have to become subtle in mind, to have a fertile intellect, be open to learning. He wasn't thinking anything so noble as helping anyone else. He just wanted to get the karmic debt monkey off his back. He felt like a slave, only thirsting for the sweetness of freedom. In karmic debt, when you owe people, they, in actual fact, own you. In ancient wisdom, it is clear that the borrower is slave to the lender. Iam realized this is the most accurate description of all the relationships he had ever had. He felt in bondage, a slave.

AL wanted to make sure that Iam and his family could never crash again, even if they experienced karmic downturns in the future in the rollercoaster of an uncertain life—he wanted to ensure that those downturns would always end with a soft landing, limit how far Iam could fall, and teach him that when you live a heavily leveraged life based on karmic debt, it is possible to fall all the way down to the depths of a living hell.

Iam started on his karmic debt elimination journey with nothing more in mind than getting rid of the pressure. What he discovered, however, went beyond his wildest dreams. The fraud of his illusive lifestyle was exposed to the bare bones of existence.

'My long-lost and now-found child. Love is the most powerful force and can take us to great heights, but unfortunately, love has been the most abused and misused force. The world needs an accurate understanding of love, because only through love will transformation occur: love for the self, love for God, and love for humanity. In truth, you can only give another what you have first given to yourself. You cannot give another something you don't have.'

Iam had never felt love for himself, only power; he had never thought of God, and with all the damage that he had done to his family, to other innocent people through his personal and business life, love for his fellow men had been nonexistent. He had earned physical wealth to the detriment of the balance in his life, and he now walked on the path of thorns, where only pain and suffering had manifested.

'My child, love is not an emotional state, but rather a transcendent state of consciousness that goes beyond the body. Love has nothing to do with bodies; love dwells in the soul. This love must flow out relentlessly and effortlessly and this is what will keep us fresh, healthy, and attractive.'

With those words, AL disappeared.

Standing in that three-square-foot telephone booth, Iam was still holding the telephone tightly to his ear, still in a state of trance.

Al's soft voice lingered and resonated, 'It is now time for you to quietly put the receiver down and drive home safely. But remember, my child, without love, all of life's treasures are locked away from you, and it is only by using the key of love that these precious jewels can be unlocked, and emerge through your vision and experiences.'

WITHOUT LOVE, ALL OF LIFE'S TREASURES ARE LOCKED AWAY FROM YOU, AND IT IS ONLY BY USING THE KEY OF LOVE THAT THESE PRECIOUS JEWELS CAN BE UNLOCKED, AND EMERGE THROUGH YOUR VISION AND EXPERIENCES.

Iam was surprised at the clarity of his mind. The negative thoughts that had previously eroded his mind now seemed to be replenished by these fresh comforting words that were taking over and replenishing his intellect. His mind was racing now. He needed to ask so many questions that he just did not know where to begin.

'How can I love myself for all the bad actions I have performed? How can I love God when I don't know God? How can I love mankind when I have done so much bad in society for my own greed?' The questions were endless.

Al's soft voice reverberated in Iam's mind, beginning to dissolve the hooks of his endless question marks: 'My sweet child, the lessons of life have just begun. You are but a traveller on the path. The choices you have made this far along your journey have brought you wealth and power... both will give you temporary, transient happiness. Now keep the faith that the choices you make for the rest of your journey will bring you imperishable treasures beyond your imagination."

'Your faith will become strong once you get to know yourself, then you will get to know me, and once you make that connection with me, I will impart knowledge of truth. Making the link, connection, or yoga (union) with me is as simple as Remembering, or Remembrance of your imperishable inheritance—it is the shortest and fastest bullet which will link you to me. It is as simple as the "A" in AL."

'Your body now needs to rest, my child. I take my leave until you are ready to make the next call.'

The irony of all of this was that it had taken a bolt of lightning to 'enlighten' Iam.

*'It is not great talents, or great learning,
or great preachers that God needs,
but men great in holiness.'*

—E. M. Bounds

Mahatma Gandhi's advice is a very deep one. It's when an angry Hindu threw a roti, the Indian cooked bread, at him and angrily demanded, 'Take it. Eat, old man', because the Mahatma ('great soul') hadn't eaten for 30 days, fasting to the death, refusing to eat unless the Hindus and Muslims refrained from the blood-thirsty civil 'war' they were engaged in at the time of partition. Gandhi had become a fragile, almost corpse-like skeleton, about to die, and the whole nation was burning, and split into two. 'Take it and eat because I don't want your death to scar my soul', he continued in anguish, 'because I took the head of a Muslim child and bashed it against a wall and crushed it to death. I saw his blood spatter all over.' Then he defiantly justified his violent act through tears of pain, claiming that was because the Muslims had raped his wife and killed his children.

An old proverb states, 'dead men tell no tales', meaning dead people will not betray any secrets. But those who have near death experiences, and are still alive to speak their truth, will reverberate with the light of pure wisdom.

The Mahatma was very quiet from his 30 days of fasting, and from the depth of his silence, he responded calmly, 'There is a way out.' The man was shocked, in disbelief, as he was traumatized, and hadn't slept for days. Gandhi said, 'There is a way out of this hell.' He said go and find a young Muslim boy who is an orphan, adopt him, and bring him up with kindness and nurture him as your own. Bring him up within your home and that will reverse the karma. But *only* make sure of one thing: make sure you bring him up as a Muslim. The man is both shocked and amazed by the profound wisdom of this act of atonement. That final 'bullet' hit home very hard because when you do something wrong, you must re-evaluate everything that went on inside of you that took you to that point. He collapses to his knees in reverence for the

Mahatma, a God-like being in whose presence he is humbled and defeated by the simple 'white flag' of surrender, to be reborn with a new paradigm of how to live a virtuous life.

Yes, there's a way out, and that is the remembrance of our original qualities, being driven accordingly to find the right path once again.

With regard to the power of love, and non-violence in action, Martin Luther King, Jr. once remarked, 'Jesus showed us the way, and Gandhi proved it could work'. The late Steven Covey also regarded Mahatma Gandhi as an extraordinary leader and likened him to a trim-tab on the rudder of a boat. The trim-tab gives us the ability to manoeuvre the boat accurately. In the same way, Gandhi was able to steer a large nation in the right direction. Currently, with a population of 1.2 billion people, that nation, India, is the largest democracy in the world.

The path of enlightenment is a long haul. It's a paradox that only when we go through many complex stages of learning are we then able to discover and reach true simplicity. One of the magic tricks of marketing is 'to simplify the complicated, and compli- cate the simple'. It's a way to keep the human mind interested. But, yes, there is a way out. In this yoga of humanity, the journey of the mind, you need iron to cut iron. You need the strength of dealing with the snakes and playing with the snakes because you can't use gold to cut iron. You need to be bulletproof in order to handle everything that's thrown at you, and ensure that you put a fortress around the original power of the soul and protect that, and express yourself accordingly.

David Gray's song 'Night Blindness' reverberates with this truth:

> Step into the silence *(go within to your original truth—Silence is the oxygen for the mind)*,
>
> Take it in your own sweet hands *(the incognito hands of good karma)*,
>
> And sprinkle it like diamonds *(share this treasury of silence and imperishable truth)*
>
> All across these lands *(everywhere)*,
>
> Blazing in the morning *(with blinding white light)*,
>
> Wearing like an iron skin *(Armour of protection in the Iron Age)*
>
> the only things worth living for are innocence and magic… *(Amen)*.

When we are armed with the three incognito tools of a spiritual warrior it will ensure success always. Firstly, with the sword of knowledge, you are armed with always performing good karma. Secondly, with the armour of humility to always be open to receiving enlightenment, and are thus always, automatically, guided and protected. Your humility is always going to keep you real. Thirdly, the shield of protection is the phenomenon of world drama. Anything can happen in the drama in the current age. There are no guarantees. The only anchor is to remain true, clean, clear, and transparent, and to be unshakable and immovable in the face of any eventuality. Karma does have undercurrents, but an honest heart can find its way out of *any maze*. It will *amaze* you, and others. When Jesus spoke of love, he even went to the extent of saying that when your worst enemy digs a sword with hatred into you, it is then you are challenged to look into the eyes of your enemy and return love. It is this very foundation of love and forgiveness from which emanated the immortal words: 'Father, forgive them, for they do not know what they do' (Luke 23:34).

> *'In the practice of tolerance, one's enemy is the best teacher.'*
>
> —DALAI LAMA

GEMS FROM THE OCEAN OF WISDOM

'To welcome an enemy is to take the opportunity to expand my heart.'

There are not many people who can accept, understand, experience, and follow that notion. One could say, 'It's a tough philosophy to follow'. But in the drama, anything can happen. That's my shield of protection. That happened, yes. But there is a way out. That reversal is there, and that's enlightenment. The switches of enlightenment go 'on', and that is why one of the *maha-mantras* ('great and pure affirmations' for delivering the mind to our 'God-self') are chanted for inviting enlightenment. To paraphrase the

Gayatri Mantra, 'We meditate on the glory of that Being who has produced this universe; may He enlighten our minds.'

It's just to enlighten the path. Let it be so bright that I make the right decisions. Let it be so bright that I will always be clear exactly how to perform the right actions, no matter the circumstances, because I will become that lighthouse of truth. That is, again, referring to CEOs and anyone worldwide. All of us need to have paths that are holistically enlightened so we make the right decisions so they don't have to go through the pain of being trapped in performing negative karma.

SIN-SEER LEADERSHIP - A SAMPLER

There are three categories of CEOs. Type 1 wants to just 'Get On' (i.e. 'cut corners'), Type 2 aims to 'Get Honest', and Type 3 excels and aims to 'Get Honours'. Type 3 is what we must all strive for: aim to 'pass with Honours' in the University of Life.

Excellence is not a skill; it is an attitude. Unity blossoms when there is appreciation of the values of each person and their special contribution. Sharing the secret of peace and happiness is great service. The simplest method of keeping people happy is to give the experience of the feeling of belonging; a sense of ownership.

Leadership is not a popularity contest, but to be a good leader you must have a big (bulletproof) heart, a clean heart, and a generous heart.

Our authenticity impacts others—it's important to make others aware of their greater potential, so they can give of themselves and benefit all. Khalil Gibran's timeless truth about giving states, 'You give but little when you give of your possessions. It is when you give of yourself that you truly give.'

The Sin-Seer leader is the ultimate Server Leader. He is clear that he can indeed insure his body with a life insurance policy, but his entire psyche is driven in the masterful art of insuring his soul. The insurance policy premium for the soul is simply good karma—good actions.

The Sin-Seer leader's focus is singular; that is, to facilitate. He focuses deeply on the formula '1+1 = 11'—collective cooperation as the most powerful synergy to bring about exponential results. The Sin-Seer leader knows that he can never teach anyone anything; people's minds are very much like our own—chaotic— like trying to organise dry sand as it slips through the fingers—but if you add the symbolic water of knowledge, it is possible to bind the sand together and build something beautiful. Everything in life is transient. This creative process is refreshed daily so that life and thought processes never become stale or ossified.

He is aware that 'training' is a term which is more apt with reference to circus animals. It is a known phenomenon that the best lion tamers have ultimately been eaten by the very lions they controlled for much of their lives.

The Sin-Seer leader attracts and interacts with beings who are driven, and open to learning. He teaches all the concepts of W.I.P.E.—remaining focused in the moment, wiping out any negativity from our yesterdays, and always living forward in the humble consciousness of *Work in Progress, Eternally*. He is aware that most people don't want to lead anything; a large percentage of people are only interested in eating ready-made bread.

In his vast experience in life with people, he estimates that 80 per cent want to 'follow the leader'; 10 per cent don't know what they want, and would very much like to live life 'backwards', in the past; only 5 per cent are true innovators; and another 5 per cent are true reformers.

Ask yourself, 'What is my truth?' Then drop all the false armour, and express what it is to be divine (your God-self), and then life opens up and you will flow and move through life dealing with all types of issues effortlessly.

Life is not a trajectory from A to B; one needs to learn to deal with mess and chaos.

'Don't lean, but rather learn', and 'Don't be mean, but rather understand the meaning of life'. Those who achieve this learn to get very passionate about everything.

One of the master keys is: Do fewer things. What are they? Those that you find most connected to your truth.

The Sin-Seer Leader has three key anchors in his life, which give him a clear sense of:

1. Identity

2. Purpose (Purpose springs from shifting of self belief: I have everything I need)

3. Direction

Without the 'underlay' of the blueprints of Sin-Seer Leadership, no leadership program is complete.

Don't just *bark* up the wrong tree, rather *embark* on your mission in life (i.e. Put your money where your mouth is).

Invest the right seeds of thought and prepare to clean up today for tomorrow.

Your company colours you. The people you meet, the books you read, whatever activity you invest yourself in will determine where you will be in your future. Listen carefully to what your current discussions are about, and this will determine the tracks you are making for your future.

Many people remain where they are, stuck with what they know—many of them in their comfort zone… zzzzzzzone. Almost asleep in it. In the era of promotion based on tenure, this was acceptable. However, in today's world, it is the formula for stagnation, personally and professionally.

Your leadership now can only be based on the principles of being a Server Leader. Does it mean that you are a servant? Many high-powered CEOs would balk at such a title. The main question is, do you Serve, or Lead? It's not a trick question! But the answer is in fact you do neither, but instead you *facilitate*—make things easier, help things to run more smoothly and effectively. This ensures a generation of strong interdependency, a collective cooperation within organisations for sure and sustained success.

You are coloured by the people you keep company with. The highest company is the company of your Creator, God. To progress in life, spend time with people who will stretch you and help you to grow, and to optimise your life physically, emotionally, intellectually, and spiritually.

Today is the age of information overload, and we are flooded with snippets of knowledge. Twitter's 140-character input is good for building breadth of information, but as Sin-Seer leaders, we need quality time to see the bigger picture, and to reflect deeply on issues.

'Most people today are "boxed in" the realm of their virtual "in-box".'

—RDM

Reduce your consumption of bite-sized *opinions* (a word which has both the words '*pins*' and '*onions*' embedded in it), and free your time so that you can read and reflect meaningfully. Understand clearly that the thought processes and actions that got you to this point in life simply won't get you to the next mountain top. It's time to ask: 'What changes do I need to make?'

In the process of inculcating the knowledge, the 'aha' or 'Eureka' moments of enlightenment, will bring to the surface all your original values. These are the original values which are required for your progressive role today. A progressive leadership career requires moving from being IQ driven—your technical expertise—to being SQ (spiritual quotient) driven (i.e. being focused on leadership behaviour, which is comprised of a different role, a transition, and a new focus). IQ focuses only on willpower and logic, but SQ focuses holistically with willpower, logic, and the true heart of understanding—a clear and powerful conscience. This then translates to one becoming a powerful visionary. It is said that vision is 100 times more powerful than willpower. However, vision without execution is hallucination. The Sin-Seer leader develops the following (*F.A.C.E.*):

1. **Rejects FALSEHOOD:** Unloads everything and anything which is not part of his truth; he keeps a 'To-Do' list, as well as a 'Not-To-Do' list

2. **Remains FOCUSED:** Stays the course, keeps the plan

   Accurate Focus has its foundation on five qualities:

   1. Vision: One hundred times more powerful than willpower

   2. Power: Eight Subtle Super Powers

   3. Speed: The Speed of Thought—Vimān—powered with high-octane fuel

   4. Strategy: Ensure that there is no 'rat' in your strategy

   5. Skill: Don't be ill, or go for the kill—have the right skill

3. **ALIGNS the Organisation:** for success based on the powerful interdependency of server leadership

4. **Keeps CONSISTENT:** Looks closely at your habits, and cultivates the best. The level of consistency also determines whether he or she is able build bridges and cultivate genuine friends, or alternatively burn bridges and cultivate transient relationships with fair-weather friends

5. **Power of EXECUTION:** The same as the power of judgement and decision-making

Many leaders are fickle, being driven by vices for short-term gain so frequently that they have difficulty finishing what they originally started based on the zeal and enthusiasm of being virtue-driven. It cripples their leadership preparation by not having the staying power long enough to learn from mistakes, master the right skills, and gain the experience needed for sustainable leadership success. One must stay with the program, as the Sin-Seer leader always prepares today for tomorrow and is always careful and carefree, but never, ever careless.

On his deathbed, Alexander the Great summoned his generals and told them his three ultimate wishes:

1. The best doctors should carry his coffin… to demonstrate that, in the face of death, even the best doctors in the world have no power to heal.

2. The wealth he has accumulated (money, gold, precious stones) should be scattered along the procession to the cemetery… in order for everybody to see that material wealth acquired on earth, stays on earth.

3. His hands should be let loose, hanging outside the coffin for all to see, so that people understand that we come to this world empty-handed and we leave this world empty-handed after the most precious treasure of all is exhausted, and that is time.

The Sin-Seer leader is able to understand clearly how to deal with the strong emotions involved in maintaining a balance with current day challenges linked to business, family, and friends, and maintaining a sound mind within a healthy body.

In a high-speed chaotic world, when people are apt to lose their mind in various whirlwind experiences, we can either explode, or implode.

We have four specific choices of response (*A.I.M.S.*):

1. *Explode with the fire of Anger*

2. *Manifest physical sicknesses and Illnesses*—Louise Hay attributes heart disease and diabetes to 'the sweetness being drained out of our lives'

3. *Implode with Mental depression*—loneliness is a symptom of communication breakdown

4. *The Sin-Seer Leader's choice is*: Become a 'detached observer'—stop and put yourself in the centre, get into the eye of the storm, remain safe, and get a better perspective. When one becomes *the detached Observer,* as opposed to the *Absorber*, one becomes insulated from the scenes of drama, and is not influenced by them. One can develop the vision to see the way forward, and can proactively use the powers within to plot that route accurately.

The Sin-Seer leader's focus on success comes from a three-stage process, bolstered by three master abilities:

STAGE 1: STAY CENTERED IN THE EYE OF THE STORM

'Who am I?'—His basic belief is clear, that he was made in the image of God.

Become centred no matter what goes on / God-self or pygmy-self—we are all born in the image of God with His original golden qualities of power, peace, truth, love, and happiness.

Stay focused, because a wandering intellect means one is not accurately connected with the team, and can deplete energy.

STAGE 2: SEE THE BIGGER PICTURE AND UNDERSTAND THE BIGGER PICTURE

'What am I supposed to be doing?'—'What are my specialties?' He is clear about the purpose / function of all concerned—no one should ever pretend to be something they are not. He is able to command a wider perspective, see the bigger picture—scene after scene. He never gets caught up or stumbles in the 'little picture'—as that is not the complete picture.

The problem is that people get stuck with little problems, and we forget that it's a scene within a scene within a scene. If you understand the big scene, you will understand the smaller scenes, but if you only relate to the little scene you cannot even begin to understand the bigger picture—which is Truth—and how things fit in within the grand scheme of things.

STAGE 3: PURPOSEFULLY JUDGE, DECIDE AND EXECUTE THE WAY FORWARD

Find your direction. What is your purpose? It's an expression of your specialty. This is your purpose and this is your direction. Once you are able to sustain yourself within the eye of the storm—in that detachment from the physical chaos, you are able to access your true inner driver—the compass to direct your outer life. You are clear as to what direction you have to take and you are accurately able to make the right *Judgement*, *Decision*, and *Execution* to ensure success.

The Sin-Seer leader does not overwhelm himself with questions of how many trillions of dollars will be required to attempt to stop the polar caps from melting or the ozone layer from depleting. He is more focused on executing his formula for success by sustaining this in his day-to-day actions. Sharing the imperishable treasures gives one happiness, and positive food for thought gives strength. Practice makes perfect.

SIN-SEER LEADER'S SUCCESS FORMULA

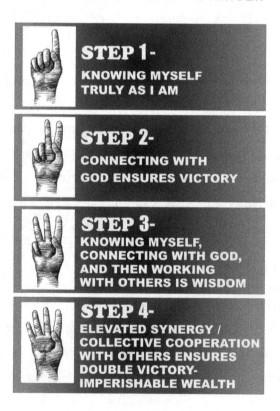

STEP 1-
KNOWING MYSELF
TRULY AS I AM

STEP 2-
CONNECTING WITH
GOD ENSURES VICTORY

STEP 3-
KNOWING MYSELF,
CONNECTING WITH GOD,
AND THEN WORKING
WITH OTHERS IS WISDOM

STEP 4-
ELEVATED SYNERGY /
COLLECTIVE COOPERATION
WITH OTHERS ENSURES
DOUBLE VICTORY-
IMPERISHABLE WEALTH

V. (2 fingers) is for Peace and Victory—When God and I become one—This brings victory.

W. (3 fingers) is for Wisdom—When I link with God, and then with others—This brings wisdom.

V.V. (4 fingers) is for Double Victory—Everyone linked together in the powerful synergy of collective cooperation—This brings double-victory—success is guaranteed as a 'Midas Touch'.

How much wisdom you have is visible on your face. Be righteous and pick up only what is good. Knowledge is a collection of facts. Wisdom is knowing how to apply knowledge. With the wisdom of collective cooperation, we are able to convert problems as high as mountains to become as soft as cotton wool in our hands. Not into small mustard seeds even, because such seeds can still cause pain if trapped under your foot in a shoe. Our clean and positive thoughts are the cure for everything. This is a great medicine.

CHAPTER EIGHT

DECIPHERING THE MEANING AND MAGIC OF WORDS

WORDZ

'W-o-r-d-z' is an enlightenment concept *coined by me* with several different aspects to it. It's a very interesting game, analysing, loosening up individual words, and reading between the lines, we are able to read between the letters, and mutate the words to extract deeper meanings from them to enlighten us. We have already used the word *soldier*. One is sold to die, when dire situations take over the world.

Let's talk about the Hindi word, Raazyukt.

Yukt is very simple. It just means 'saturated'. *Raaz* means 'secrets'. Saturated with secrets. And so many words are like this.

> *"For last year's words belong to last year's language,*
> *And next year's words await another voice."*
>
> —T.S. Eliot, Four Quartets

Like, growing pains; are you all *grown up* ('God-self') or are you all *groans* ('pygmy-self')? While growing up, it's easy to just groan. Or, are you ready for the seed to evolve and grow in its natural way? This is in the context of what Khalil Gibran said about the pygmy-self and the God-self. Sure, people are all grown up physically, but some are stunted emotionally, and have a heart the size of a Pygmy. They forget their God-self. They forget those original qualities of the Supreme Being within them. They don't grow up. It's just groans.

Another word is *rats*. The word *Laboratory* contains the word *rat*. There are always rats being used in laboratories for testing purposes. I know someone studying for her PhD in a famous British university, though she is squeamish, she reluctantly accepted the 'licence to kill' a total of 25 rats by holding their neck, and sharply tugging at their tails, and snapping their spines. Of course, it is all specifically for experimental purposes.

However, let's study the word *Enlightenment*, which has the word *light* in it. Clarity brings peace of mind, which also *lightens* any weight of burdens of the mind. When someone switches on a *light* in the room, *any* rats and cockroaches scurry away. That is what happens within the landscape of the mind when it's *enlightened*. Those rats that are eating away at you without you knowing, they are dispelled the moment the light comes on. One needs to constantly keep a check to ensure there is no *rat* in their *Strategy*. This will ensure that the mind is free of any and all cobwebs.

Another word is *umbilical cord* and the foetus. The umbilical *cord* is like the *cord* of *cordiality*. The *cord* of the bondages, and also *chords* of music that keep us connected. The chords of music blow the dust off of the soul. It is a shortcut to connecting with your higher being.

In decision-making, it's like a *train* of thought, a *train* of thought station, and missing your train, and training ground, and the lesson. What *train* are you on, which station are you at? Are you missing the *train*? Who is your *locomotive* (train of thought) driver? Is his *motive*—loco (mad), or is it sound?

When discussing 'trains of thought', let's look at the school of Absurd Drama. This is drama which aims to enlighten through absurdity. It is based on existential thought that emphasizes the absurdity of human existence by employing disjointed, repetitious, and meaningless dialogue, purposeless and confusing situations, and plots that lack realistic or logical development. Sometimes, the dialogue is referred to as 'Pinteresque', from Harold Pinter's plays. A similar absurdity is reflected in Monty Python's Flying Circus TV series. It's based on the premise that I speak ten words and you pick up only three, and seven go over your head, which is often the case in a conversation. You respond to those three and you respond with 10 words. I miss seven of them, take only three, and then a mass of miscommunication happens that evolves into this drama that is simply 'absurd'. How does decision-making become absurd? Yet we see it all around us, when you look at big organizations, and wonder exactly how did they make those wrong decisions? The speed of the world today, and the deluge of data available at our fingertips, can convert our lives into an absurd drama. Crowded House, in 'Don't Dream It's Over', state,

'There is freedom within, there is freedom without', and indeed, sometimes we 'try to catch the deluge in a paper cup'.

Language and words all vie to communicate. Almost 35 years ago, we studied the phenomenon of 'jive talking' in sociology, and understood that it had life as a language of its own. At that time, we were taught that it's not the 'Queen's English', but it is relevant for those who use it for communication. Words are so malleable that you can decipher them, spell, misspell them, and turn them back-to-front to squeeze a fresh meaning out of them. Words can be like spells, magic spells, and can be used to 'dispel' negativity. Like *Solutions* can also be *'Soul Lotions'*, which can soothe any negative situation or condition.

That's the very beautiful thing about all the words that I have coined. I have within my mind a veritable treasury of words and wordz which help me to swim constantly in an ocean of answers. With this sampler, I hope to create that inspiration in others to break down words, and share them. I always love to know the origin of the words, and then twist them and find much deeper meanings.

When using the word pygmy, it is not used in any way to demean the pygmy race, but rather just to refer to the smallness of size; this is most certainly the perspective with which Khalil Gibran used the term.

When using *wordz* you can further clarify the phenomenon of the pygmy-self versus the God-self. The pygmy-self is basic, *'selfish'*, *'Sellers of Fish'*, *'S.illy ELF'*, wanting a 'tit-for-tat' mercantile return for every action they perform. Even in exchanging emotions, it's an 'I'll scratch your back, if you scratch mine', and that relates to all the *'mine'* fields within the psyche which can explode at any time. U2's song 'One' poses the question, 'Have you come here (for me) to play Jesus to the lepers in your head?' The lepers are symbolic of the explosive 'minefields'. The beings who are driven by the God-self are the wisdom keepers, who are in the golden mold of 'Fishers of Men'.

For instance, when you say 'recap', recap is increasing your 'cap'acity, and 'cap'ability. As a leader, does the 'cap size' fit, or are you going to 'capsize' your organization?

Practice makes perfect. It's the power of *introspection and analysis* which helps one to absorb the knowledge and take ownership of the same for sharing with others. After *absorbing the knowledge*, this is a treasury of words that remains within you. But a treasury is not something that you keep locked away in your mental Fort Knox, which you just keep looking at everyday, saying, 'Oh, I've amassed so much fortune. Oh, it's lovely.' The treasury is to be shared, because as love is multiplied when it is shared, these words, this technique, this mechanism, is only multiplied when it is shared.

'Sinning' literally means missing the target. What is the target? When teaching the skills of archery, the great Brahmin warrior Dronacharya, put Arjuna and his clan to the test. He had placed on one of the trees a wooden bird with a prominently painted eye.

He addressed all the students, "Young princes, what is the target and what do you see?"

The first pupil, Yudhishtra replied, "I can see the bird, the tree, the fruits on the tree and more birds." The second, Duryodhana, replied, "I can see the bird, the tree, the leaves, the fruits, another bird..." The third, Bhima, "I too can see the bird, the tree, the fruits...."

Next was the turn of the twins, Nakula, "I can see the people, the trees and the bird" and Sahadeva, "I can see the bird, the fruits and the tree." Finally, it was the turn of Arjuna, who with perfect concentration and focus stated "I can see only the pupil of the eye of the bird, and nothing else." Dronacharya finally smiled and said, "Fire!" and Arjuna let loose the arrow which found its mark. Dronacharya turned to the other princes and said, "Did you all understand the point of this test? When you aim for something, you must look at nothing else but the target. Only intense concentration can help you strike the target.

That is how focused you can be on the target. Whatever your sins may have been, there is nothing to be feared. Basically you have gone to the realm of the vices that are within. The virtues, the treasury, are all there. These words are like secrets that are all within, that are revealed to you. When you use them and you remain true to your original qualities, you are then back to being accurate, hitting the target.

There are three master targets given to you. *Om* means, very simply, *I am*, like our character Iam. We have *Om Shanti*, which is 'I am an original being of peace'. *Om Kushi* is 'I am a being of happiness'. And *Om Anand*, 'I am a being of bliss'. These qualities exist within everyone. Once we are able to access our original peace, happiness, and bliss, we need to keep centred in these original qualities. This knowledge is revealed to us in three forms; when mastered, we become 'saturated' with the wisdom to become a 'lighthouse' to guide ourselves and others through life.

Our aim is to become (1) *Yukti-Yukt* (Saturated with the Methods), (2) *Raaz-Yukt* (Saturated with the Deep Secrets of the Knowledge), and (3) *Yog-Yukt* (Saturated in Union with God). One of the *yuktis*

I use, even in my business world, is that we go on a one-minute 'positive' silence break and everybody must be totally relaxed. Silence is the oxygen for the mind. Tension creates untruth, sinning, missing the target. If you can remain calm, peaceful, and content, then it is easy for you to always share the truth.

This can be likened to when the truth drug is administered to someone. What is the truth serum? It is an intense relaxant. Sodium thiopental, also known as sodium pentothal (by Abbott Labs), is a rapid-onset, short-acting barbiturate general anaesthetic. Ironically, it is also usually the first of three drugs administered during most lethal injections in the United States. When you're totally relaxed, you will always speak the truth. Therefore, you always hit the target. It's when you're holding on to all those negatives that you're missing the target. The word *Aim* also has the name Iam in it, and also MIA (missing in action), like a POW imprisoned without a trace. There is disturbance where there is turbulence, '*peacelessness*', and storms of chaos. Clarity brings about a peace of mind. When things are unclear, you become peaceless, and then sure to make the wrong decisions.

The solution is to become introspective. Go into the eye of the storm. This is the third eye, we call it, the divine eye within. When I mention *yuktiyukt*, these are methodologies of keeping things calm. There are many *yuktis* (methods) that keep you on track, and these are the methodologies of staying on track. One of the keys is going into the eye of the storm because the storm that is brewing in the world doesn't allow you to stay centred. So once you stay centred within, you are able to find that inner compass that will direct your outer life and bring out the leader within you.

So the methods of remaining constantly in higher conscious-ness enable you to stay close to that which is true, because, in reality, there's only one faithful companion who stays with you throughout your travels in this great journey called life, and that is Truth. Truth is a companion that can never leave you. Sometimes, the pathways are very steep. Staying true is being true to those original qualities and silently helping you to navigate through all the storms of life. It doesn't have to be a noisy way of doing things. Dissolving negativity is all to do with staying true, staying with the truth. Again, it is likened to a dolphin creating a whirlwind or a kind of tornado effect around Iam when he's in that deep ocean and goes into himself. When you go into yourself, remember, it's the realm of the spiritual quotient, that SQ.

Having a high IQ (Intelligence Quotient) is greatly valued in the world today. However, when IQ is used in trying to control someone's emotions, it really can be a whirlwind experience. Being only driven by a high IQ breeds arrogance, which opens the doorway to falsehood, whereas a higher level of SQ emanates natural humility, which ensures that you are always in the realm of truth. IQ can 'absorb' negativity while trying to solve a problem. SQ uses the power to 'observe, and not absorb' to find accurate solutions. When you can stay centred and you know that the true heartbeat of the soul is guiding you, that's what can really help solve problems.

The key principles and methodologies which keep the satellite navigation 'Satnav' of the Soul, always on the right 'track' are as following: the first is *to observe and not absorb*. It's like a bird compared to an ant. When you get a bird's eye view on matters you can solve them. You don't get caught by the gravitational pull of the earth, and thereby get caught in the negative. You don't keep eating away at a leaf like an ant completely unaware the next minute it's going to be crushed.

The second is *be aware but not judgmental*. See, but don't see. Hear, but don't hear. Be aware of all realities, even the negative, but don't become judgmental, or a *mental judge*. With your awareness and acceptance, you allow the breathing space for the other to change from negative to positive. The third is *step in, step out*. Like a gardener who plants. He steps in, removes the weeds and parasites, but he doesn't hang around yelling at the plants to 'grow, grow, grow'. He respectfully *steps in, and steps out*. Perform your function, play your part accurately, and then let nature respectfully take its course.

The fourth is *to focus and to flow*. When we look at the phenomenon of time—this is a result of a harmonized rhythmic spinning of the Earth (flow) and its relationship with the fixed sun (focus). The sun gives light (focus) and the Earth holds the potential to 'flower'; both focus and flow are required for accurate functioning. In life and the work situation, accurate focus is when we collectively have all three: (1) Willpower, (2) Thought (logic), and (3) (the heart of) understanding in one focused point to optimize results. Both 'over-focus' and 'over-flowing' are negative. Accurate discernment is required to achieve optimum results.

The fifth is *the collective and the individual*. Like birds that fly out over the winter season to a warmer climate, they have a method that they use. The leader is not the leader all the time when they're flying and they have a formation where they can change positions. That's what a server leader does. Does he serve or does he lead?

Some cry out, 'I'm not a servant. I want to be a leader'. Some leaders are as heavy as lead. But the key point that today's Server Leader must understand is that one does not need to 'to serve or lead', but to facilitate. To facilitate is to make life easy for all in the common goal of success for one and all. Simply put, 'success is not success without a successor'.

The sixth, one of the greatest, is the *principle of faith*. It's like a pole vaulter. You use all the knowledge, like a pole vaulter. You run up, and at an appropriate point, you pin the pole firmly on the ground and jump, and there is a point at which you have to let the pole go. Otherwise, you are not able to make the jump, that leap of faith. He has to let go of the very thing that helped prop him up and then make that jump. Faith can be likened to driving a car: you also don't need to know all of the mechanisms of a car before you go in, turn on the ignition and drive it. Or if you want to reach the twelfth floor of a building, you pop into a lift and press a button and you get there. That's how the mechanism of faith works. Faith is a function of understanding. The personification of faith states, *'I may not see the picture right now, but I am willing for the picture to become clearer and complete later.'* If the destination becomes hazy, I have to stay stable, and not fluctuate—this is only possible through deep faith and love for God. It is what allows one to 'remain in the eye' of any storm. These are some of the principles and methods of remaining in the higher consciousness.

SONGZ—MY PATHWAYS TO THE SOUL THROUGH ROCK AND ROLL

'When will it be possible for rock and roll to bring a positive transformation in the world? Only when the world realises songs that touch the soul connects us to the Divine, thereby emerging our original qualities of peace, love, truth, happiness, and bliss.'

—RDM

It's my personal experience that there are songs which unlock the gateways to the soul, songs that touch the higher self, the God-self, and unlock the eternal inner being. In trying to express such experiences, which are like epiphanies, a deluge of words can drown anyone, and one may never experience my sharing without experimenting for oneself. In Staind's song 'Epiphany', he claims, 'So I speak to you in riddles,' cause my words get in my way'. Words can make one stumble in the art of communicating the truth; however, the vibration of music is able to communicate without such stumbling blocks.

Songs that touch the soul make for 'Easy Yoga', the instant access to becoming detached, and being in touch with your inner being, which is then able to have a higher experience in the realm of their 'God-self', before you are able to interact with others. Harmony is represented by an equilateral triangle. It's having that deep recognition of your original self, the recognition of a Higher Being, our Creator, and then we come into interaction with others, to whom we give recognition.

'Music washes away from the soul
the dust of everyday life.'

—BERTHOLD AUERBACH

'Without music, life would be a mistake.'

—FRIEDRICH WILHELM NIETZSCHE

'Music is by far the best and
purest drug in the world.'

—MOTHERJANE—INDIAN ROCK BAND

'To understand emotion and connect
with God, one requires no language.'

—RICHA SHARMA SHLOK—SUFI SINGER

'There is nothing in the world so
much like prayer as music is.'

—WILLIAM P. MERRILL

'Music's the medicine of the mind.'

—JOHN A. LOGAN

'Music is an outburst of the soul.'

—FREDERICK DELIUS

At times, I say to people, 'Look, I respect you more than you can ever respect yourself because you're not truly aware of who you are'. Respect is based on the awareness that everyone has value.

'People will do anything, no matter how absurd, to avoid facing their own souls.'

—CARL JUNG

The common definition of an atheist is one who does not believe in the existence of God. However, an alternative definition is that an atheist is one who does not know God. Lack of God in one's life breeds negativity. I can say this with conviction, because I actually went through a phase during my 'absurd drama' days, when I studied Jean-Paul Sartre's *Nausea*, in which the protagonist is totally 'sick' with the realm of his existence in the world. Over time, his disgust towards existence forces him into self-hatred and near-insanity.

'You are the music while the music lasts.'

—T.S. ELIOT

Without the filament of God, the experience of pessimism is like being locked in a suffocating black box, a dark room, with no windows or doors, yet we're waiting for some being to open the non-existent door from outside. Take Samuel Beckett's *Waiting for Godot*, where a couple of forlorn tramps are just 'killing time' and waiting 'in slow motion' for a being named Godot, who never shows up. I've experienced that phase in my life, and can endorse that this false paradigm can intoxicate one into believing it to be real. The mind-set that is fixated with only two important or valid events, birth and death, is all that's important. The rest, the gap between birth and death, is for mindless Pavlovian purposeless games we play from the 'cradle to the grave'.

Only true intimacy can destroy these habitual games we play, and thereby make our relationships real, and lives purposeful. The end of Edward Albee's *Who's Afraid of Virginia Woolf* depicts this perfectly in the film, when the dysfunctional couple played by Richard Burton and Elizabeth Taylor experience a breakdown during an overly tense evening, when their relationship based on their games of falsehood is purged and they find genuine relief in rediscovering the truth, and their original intimacy.

Unlocking the limited paradigm from the linear birth–death, and discovering the eternal cycle of life, opens the doorways to this higher experience. This is like an ignition to your higher self, sparking the ignition of the soul. When we look at examples, like 'Free Bird' by Lynyrd Skynyrd, or 'Child in Time' by Deep Purple, it's very accurate when it says, 'Sweet child in time, you'll see the line.' The line. What line is that? Use your *divine vision* to perceive the *divine division*, the line that's drawn between good and bad. The accurate lesson is given to the blind man shooting at the world. What makes a man blind? He doesn't have the third divine eye that can see what he's doing.

There are many songs which can express this.

'Stairway to Heaven' by Led Zeppelin encompasses it all. What are our shadows? It's those shadows, those vices, those personifications of vices, those I-shadows, those me-shadows. The negative ego, I.

This relates to what I was discussing about the spiritual principles and methodology, in that there's something absolutely perfect about the eight powers that also emerge within this practice. One is the experience with the music.

What is the real stairway to heaven is very simple. It's basically being true to your inner being of virtues, those original virtues which take you to heaven or heavenly experiences.

If we are lucky, in life, we can have access to a mentor who enlightens us like a piper or a flautist playing the song of truth which enters our consciousness to carve our way forward forever on an enlightened path. Remember, the flutist is Krishna, the greatest prince of princes, and flautist from the Golden Age, who charmed everyone into dancing the eternal and tireless dance of truth. Then there's also the Pied Piper of Hamlin—the one who uses the flute to 'musically charm' the rats who were tormenting the city, and gets rid of them by leading them to a canal away from the city where they drown themselves. What is *reason*? It's like the *real son*. You're the 'real son' of God. The reason is because you live and are driven by reason. It is *illusion* that makes one *ill*.

That oneness tells me that what's in me and in you is exactly the same. When that unity is created, that's when we can become a 'rock' and 'not to roll'. Bob Dylan's 'Like a Rolling Stone' is a very caustic song where he states that you've got an ego so high that you will suffer the karmic consequences 'like a rolling stone'. The very essence of this song is euphoric in that he makes it pleasurable to detach, and shed the skin of falsehood.

You've probably heard the song 'You're Beautiful', which is one which touches the core of the soul. James Blunt, the singer, was asked in an interview, 'Isn't that the most overplayed track ever?' It's caused so many breakups, so much pain, so much closeness between couples, that they became 'too close for comfort' and didn't want to hear it anymore. He (perhaps jokingly) retorted, 'Well, it still gets me laid.' So with that blasé comment, he *somewhat* belittled everything that song was made for, that total perfection of love, the definition of love. Nonetheless, James Blunt, a perennial superstar, played his part in creating a masterpiece which touches the soul, in line with Andrew Marvell's *Definition of Love*, where the path of true love runs on parallel lines, and as such the two lovers in pure and perfect love with each other can never unite physically.

Throughout this chapter, and indeed throughout the book, I have used *examples from Hindi, English and classic rock*. We don't often think about how there are so many double meanings in words and in songs. These *double entendres* are around us, and it's through these double meanings that we can find guidance in life. If we listen closely, both to ourselves and to the meaning of the words around us, we will always find the true meaning and true guidance. If you think about it, truth is the key to your inner treasury, the real you inside. The messages for that are all around you. You must develop the power to experience, churn, and decipher the meanings for yourself.

It's like being the Jackie Chan of spirituality. Jackie Chan uses every little thing as a weapon. If it comes in front of him, he uses it as a weapon. To be the Jackie Chan of spirituality means that you use every situation and every moment, find the benefit, learn from it, and move on. With practice it materializes as habit. Because you develop it, it happens naturally. It doesn't matter what situation you're in. You're interacting with somebody, and you're automatically linked in at a much deeper level. By interacting only physically, and denying the interaction of heart, mind, and soul, you're cheating yourself in the process.

The experience of songs throughout life has been an amazing soundtrack to my existence. Of course, I've been to hard and soft rock concerts and enjoyed my fair share of headbanging at the university's 'Headbangers Ball', to the likes of Black Sabbath's 'Paranoia', Deep Purple's 'Smoke on the Water', Steppenwolf's 'Born to Be Wild', and the list of my favourites goes on *ad infinitum*, including punk rock, disco, you name it. I've been through it all. I can sit peacefully and they still affect me. Even the absolute current, up-to-date stuff, I can still pick stuff out from there and it affects me in a particular way. I can tell you straight away if a song can get to me—if it touches my soul—or not.

Whether it's Evanescence's 'Bring Me to Life', Linkin Park feat. Jay-Z's 'Numb Encore', Pink Floyd's 'The Wall', or Sufi music—you name it—I have an ear for it. I have a feel for it. It takes me. I've been told that I have an eclectic ear. If it is a transient song, fine. It may hit me, but within a couple of plays it's worn out. It's not a permanent fixture. If it doesn't touch your heart and the heartbeat of your soul, this is not going to make any sense to you. I'm sharing my personal experiences which have touched me. As discussed earlier, it is in the sharing of experiences that one is able to enlighten. In that vein, you can rest assured that there are millions of books in the pipeline by people wanting to share their experiences through "new' self-help books; the 99 cent self-help books. The key is for the reader to develop the power to discern and have his or her own personal experience and grow from it.

ESSENTIAL TRACKS

Experience euphoria, enlightenment, and transformation from your pygmy-self to God-self. The experience of the best *Melodies* enable you to *mellow* and *die alive*. What it means by die alive is you've killed that negativity within you and you are privileged to be in this moment and this life.

To 'die alive', very simply, refers to 'killing all that is negative within you' and being driven with your higher self and losing yourself in the music to let your mind dance the dance of truth, so it can truly dance on the heads of snakes. It's a war against *maya* or illusion, falsehood.

Access these songs, listen, and experience them through the light of my perception of them.

'FIGHT THE GOOD FIGHT'—TRIUMPH

The days grow shorter and the nights are getting long
(*Darkness of the Iron Age*)

Feels like we're running out of time
(*Speed of the world today*)

Every day it seems much harder tellin' right from wrong
(*The power of discernment is depleted*)

You got to read between the lines
*(Use techniques to fragment the deluge of data
and be able to discern the truth)*

Don't get discouraged, don't be afraid
*(Don't lose the heartbeat of the soul—conscience;
and to stay with truth —be fearless)*

We can make it through another day,
make it worth the price we pay
The Good Book says it's better to give than to receive
(Mastery of Karma / The more you give the more you receive)

I do my best to do my part
(Your personal best)

Nothin' in my pockets; I got nothin' up my sleeve
(Nothing to Hide, purity, transparency, honesty and clarity)

I keep my magic in my heart
(The magic of having a clean and clear conscience)

Keep up your spirit, keep up your faith, baby
(Remain soul conscious and strong Faith)

I am counting on you, you know what you've got to do
(You are your own best judge)

Fight the good fight every moment, every
minute every day—It's your only way
All your life you've been waiting for your
chance—Where you'll fit into the plan
But you're the master of your own destiny—
So give and take the best that you can
You think that a little more money
can buy your soul some rest
You better think something else instead—You're
so afraid of being honest with yourself

You'd better take a look inside your head—
Nothing is easy, nothing good is free
But I can tell you where to start—
Take a look inside your heart
There's an answer in your heart
(*Conscience—the heartbeat of the soul*)

'Hide' by Creed

(*Hyde-Skin-Shed the skin of Body Consciousness
and liberate yourself with truth*)

To what do I owe this gift, my friend?
My life, my love, my soul?
I've been dancing with the devil way too
long, and it's making me grow old
Let's leave… oh, let's get away—Get lost in time
Where there's no reason left to hide—
Let's leave… oh let's get away
Run in fields of time—Where there's no reason left to hide
No reason to hide—What are you going
to do with your gift, dear child?
Give life, give love, give soul? Divided is the one who dances
For the soul is so exposed—So exposed
Let's leave… oh, let's get away—Get lost in
time—Where there's no reason left to hide

'Child in Time' by Deep Purple

Sweet child, in time you'll see the line
(*with the divine eye of knowledge*)

The line that's drawn between good and the bad
(*The power of discernment*)

See the blind man shooting at the world
(*CEOs in the world today*)

Bullets flying, taking toll

(generating sorrow, like 'friendly fire' killing your own troops)

If you've been bad, lord I bet you have
(In the Iron Age, it easy to perform negative karma)

And you've not been hit by flying lead
(If karma hasn't caught up with you yet)

You'd better close your eyes
(Close your physical eyes)

Bow your head…Wait for the ricochet
(Be merciful to yourself, and with humility open your divine eye, and…wait for the ricochet…)

(The Conscience cries out)

Oh, god, oh, no don't, oh, ain't gonna do it, oh, no, no, no

'FIRE FALL DOWN' BY HILLSONG UNITED

I'll never be the same
No, I'll never be the same
'Cause I know that you're alive
You came to fix my broken life
And I'll sing to glorify
Your Holy name, Jesus Christ.

You've changed it all
You broke down the wall
When I spoke and confessed
In you I am blessed
Now I walk in the light
In victorious sight of you.

Fire fall down
Fire fall down
On us we pray
As we seek
Fire fall down
Your fire fall down

On us we pray.

Show me your heart
Show me your way
Show me your glory.

'IT'S YOUR LOVE' BY TIM MCGRAW / FAITH HILL

(Can be likened to a Euphoric Sufi song)

It's your love
It just does somethin' to me
It sends a shock right through me
I can't get enough
And if you wonder
About the spell I'm under
It's your love

Better than I was
More than I am
And all of this happened
By takin' your hand

And who I am now
Is who I wanted to be
And now that we're together
I'm stronger than ever
I'm happy and free

"GIVE ME YOUR EYES" BRANDON HEATH

Looked down from a broken sky
Traced out by the city lights
My world from a mile high
Best seat in the house tonight
Touched down on the cold black top
Hold on for the sudden stop
Breathe in the familiar shock
Of confusion… And chaos

All those people goin' somewhere
Why have I never cared?

Give me Your eyes for just one second
Give me Your eyes so I can see
Everything that I keep missing
Give me Your love for humanity
Give me Your arms for the broken-hearted
The ones that are far beyond my reach
Give me Your heart for the ones forgotten
Give me Your eyes so I can see

Step out on a busy street
See a girl and our eyes meet
Does her best to smile at me
To hide what's underneath
There's a man just to her right
Black suit and a bright red tie
Too ashamed to tell his wife
He's out of work, he's buyin' time

All those people goin' somewhere
Why have I never cared?

I've been there a million times
A couple of million eyes
Just move and pass me by
I swear I never thought that I was wrong

Well I want a second glance
So give me a second chance
To see the way You've seen the people all along

Give me Your Eyes (Give me Your eyes for just one second)
Lord, give me Your eyes (Give me Your eyes so I can see)
Everything (Everything that I keep missing)
(Give me Your love for humanity)
Give me Your heart (Give me Your
arms for the broken-hearted)
For the broken hearted (The ones that
are far beyond my reach)
Give me Your heart (Give me Your
heart for the ones forgotten)
Lord, give me Your eyes (Give me Your eyes so I can see)

DMX's 'Gon' Give It to Ya (Clean Version)' is a perfect example of being at war with illusion on that spiritual battlefield. Other examples are Tom Petty's 'Don't You Come Around Here No More', and Bad Company's 'Bad Company'. Only iron can cut iron. These are experiences of songs. In supreme union, or yoga, you have 'Silent Lucidity' by Queensryche. Other examples are 'Come into the Light' and 'Naked' by Bliss, 'The Spirit of Radio' by Rush, 'Feel' by Robbie Williams, and 'A Case of You' by Joni Mitchell. The nature of *maya* / illusion is expounded in 'My, Oh My' by David Gray and 'Building a Mystery' by Sarah McLachlin.

Sting evokes the golden past and golden future's cycle of life in *Fields of Gold*. He makes a promise from the core of his soul that, 'In the days still left / I swear we'll walk in fields of gold'. What this implies is that 'I will never be driven by the vices in my relationship with you. In the days still left, I swear, we'll walk in fields of gold'. That's a very deep, touching song which has the power to transform one who truly listens and experiences it in the depth of its wisdom.

Other big ones are Dire Straits's 'Sultans of Swing', all euphoric songs, with 'Higher Love' by Stevie Winwood, and 'Little Pink Houses' by John Mellencamp.

Of course, for detachment, you have 'Cuts Like A Knife' by Bryan Adams, 'Say Goodbye' by Triumph, 'Free Fallin' by Tom Petty, and 'Knockin' On Heaven's Door' by Eric Clapton. The urgency of the moment in changing is like 'Now' by Van Halen, 'Ordinary Man' by Triumph, and 'Fight the Good Fight' by Triumph.

Then euphoric anthems, like 'Paradise City' by Guns N Roses, 'Baba O'Riley' by The Who, 'Feel Like Makin' Love' by Bad Company, 'For What It's Worth' by Buffalo Springfield, amongst many others.. From Sarah McLachlan, a song called 'Into the Fire', and 'Songbird' by Fleetwood Mac.

These are just a handful. There are innumerable songs which have the ability to make you think more profoundly, once you experience them spiritually.

CHAPTER NINE

POLISHING THE JEWEL THAT IS YOU

'Polishing the jewel that is you' is about how all of these experiences, all of these challenges that people go through in life, polish you. It's like a diamond. The more a diamond is cut, the more brilliantly it shines.

Though the journey is through time itself, the cycle of time is eternal. The greatest teachers are responsibility and experience and what that does to you. The moment one takes responsibility, one becomes a leader.

Your soul will remember the terrain of this book as you traverse through it, and your conscience will nod in agreement with each jewel of knowledge as it emerges from deep within your original self. Music blows the dust off your soul. Music which truly touches the soul moves faster than a speeding bullet to detach you from negativity, and help you to transcend to the realm of your original truth within.

In this journey through time, we could have a map and many self-help books. In this book, however, we're sharing the map. And we are also saying that the journey is through time itself. We have a protagonist who is here, who is reborn only to experience even more of life. It's a reflection of your own journey.

This cycle of time never ceases. You can continue to evolve yourself into becoming an authority, a genuine, humble authority on what truth is, what reality is, what life is about, and maximizing your personal potential.

Where there's a will there's a way. I had a character *in the original conceptual stages* of my book who was a palmist and I called him *My Pal Mistry*. He's my pal because he dispels the mystery of life, and allows me to get self-sovereignty / mastery of my life. My Palmistry, My Pal Mistry. When applying Wordz, it's like doing '*Laps*' in the great Olympic size swimming pool of life, and then using the '*slaps*' of life to make them your '*pals*'. You turn it around and you make them your pals. You make them your friends and you grow from every experience there is. The map is not the journey. The journey is personal, unique, and has to be embarked upon *by* every individual being who cares about living life to the fullest. It depends on your inner seed and how it flowers.

But in terms of potential, how much do we water it with knowledge? How much do we inculcate? How much do we nurture it with minerals, the fertility of the soil and fertility of the mind? To how much light do we expose it? 'Fools in their madness all around know that the light don't sleep.' That's a line from David Gray's song 'Silver Lining'. The light is the light of God and the light of enlightenment. It's true, it never sleeps, and it's there for everyone as an equal opportunity. It all depends on how much light you want to absorb, and what your capacity is, not only for holding onto the imperishable jewels of knowledge, but also your capacity for sharing it.

It depends on you and your journey, how much willpower you have to say, 'I will do it'. When you take the first step you become a visionary, being able to use willpower, logic, and understanding of the heart in one single focus, to bring dreams into your eternal reality, in your imperishable reality. Forever and a day. If you can perceive this, you will be a master achiever. A lot of organizations and a lot of people think, 'Yes, I have the willpower and the logic.' They have the iron rod and the carrot and stick approach. But what they actually have is the iron rod that they (metaphorically) beat people on the head with.

If you're only driven by willpower and logic, that's not enough. You must add this huge heart of understanding. Even within the palm of your hand, I'm able to see accurately the strength of your willpower, the level of your logic and the amount of understanding in your heart. That's one focused hit. Within focus, you have to have vision, power, speed, strength, and strategy. When you bring it into an accurate focus with balance, there are some people who have too much willpower, very little logic, and they have a good understanding. But if they ever mix with the wrong type of people, they will have the willpower to do the wrong things because they will be guided negatively. They don't have the logic to break it down and understand it for themselves.

This is a very deep point. But if you know and understand who you are, you will surround yourself with correct beings. You will have the power to attract those who will help you to grow. The reason why willpower, logic and understanding of the heart are different in all beings is because they've had different experiences and different cycles in their lives. Even within the palm, the line of the heart, if I look at some people's hands is very cut up. They've had some very heavy experiences that have carved into their heart. That is why when people have a **bad** experience, they say things like, 'I'm gutted.' Gutted like a fish. They have an experience that carves them up.

This is reflected in the palm of the hand. After his initial arrest and incarceration by the British in South Africa, Gandhi had a palmist friend who told him, 'You're going to die in this jail'.

This friend never thought that Gandhi, having been educated in England, would become so deeply spiritual and true to himself. He would evolve and develop pure and powerful leadership traits in handling the extreme circumstances which tested him. The lines of his hands started changing. The palmist was stunned. Every single moment there's an inflection. There's a change going on in your being. Everything, even reading this book, is part of your journey. It's changing you.

> *'The weak can never forgive—forgiveness is the attribute of the strong.'*
>
> —Mahatma Gandhi

If you're in agreement to take that journey in your mind, the mind's eye, and find out who you really are, that's when your greatest dreams can have an eternal reality. You only ever get what you deserve, never what you desire. Sow the seeds, see the seeds that you sow. Every single day. Every single moment. The deepest seeds are our inner thoughts. Keep your thoughts positive, clean, and clear, and these seeds will clear the path of thorns, and germinate the best fruits will germinate in the garden of your life.

This is polishing the jewel that's within you. Don't worry about the garbage of the world. There's going to be a lot, lot more that you're going to see. But use those principles / powers to observe, and don't absorb, 'see, but don't see', 'hear, but don't hear'. Be aware of all realities, but never become like a heavily laden sponge; instead, remain detached, light, and nimble. Know them for what they are. Use your powers.

YOUR EIGHT SUPERPOWERS

GEMS FROM THE OCEAN OF WISDOM

'Mastery of the senses gives you eyes that see through things, ears that hear the heart of things, and lips that only speak the essence of things.'

As your jewel gets polished, you develop eight super powers. Those super powers are very simple.

1. **Power to Merge:** Allows unworthy feelings and emotions to be dissolved by God's light and love—leaving us with feelings of compassion, no matter what the situation or behaviour of others. Put a 'full stop' and pack up'.

   You are able to *pack up* in a second. You are able to put a full stop to all negativity, and focus *accurately*—in one second, because the power of the 'full stop' is the master power. It's not a comma; it's not a question mark that's going to hook you upside down like a fish on the end of a hook. It's a full stop. It has the authority to say 'time out', and stop play. You'll recognize that little dot within that is your soul and you go into it. You withdraw.

2. **Power to Withdraw:** (From negativities within and without). To let go and detach. To become an observer. This is the foundation of a great server leader—the Sin-Seer Leader. You are able to withdraw and observe the outer world. That full stop is your power to pack up all negativity, like a turtle going into its shell and using its shell as an outer protection. He goes in and he's able to reflect and take stock in there and, under the shell of protection, he can really observe what's going on around him.

   When these first two powers begin working for us—our head and heart become healthier. This is the basis for the next two powers:

3. **Power to Tolerate:** When tolerance begins to operate as a power, it is people around us who notice. We ourselves

are hardly aware of it. We are not affected by stones being thrown at us. We remain untroubled and, effortlessly, continue to give of our 'fruits'—the healthy thoughts and feelings that come from our innate goodness.

You're not snapped in half by the world around you. The power to tolerate is like a fruit tree that gives a mango fruit even though a rock is chucked at it. Sometimes life is like that. You have to bend and sway and remain flexible. Otherwise, you will be snapped in half.

4. **Power to Accommodate / Adjust**: This power allows us to flow with life, to take in stride life's many twists and turns, without ever losing our focus or compromising our aim.

    To adjust, so that any difference in the world makes no difference to me. Think of a swimming pool. You throw a brick in it and the water doesn't ask any questions. The water just adjusts. You have so much knowledge and you just adjust. When you've become an ocean is when you throw anything and the ocean just accepts it, swallows it up. It just adjusts. It doesn't make any difference; you're an ocean.

5. **Power of Discernment**: The ability to know clearly the difference between right and wrong, to see clearly. To use a microscope. What are the microbes? The negativity of the world. Say, 'No. I will be driven by the light. I will be driven by the truth'. For instance, politicians can 'sex up' documents in order to enter wars. Why would they

'sex up' those documents? That's because they haven't got their microscope on. They haven't got the discernment power to see right from wrong. The discernment power is very simple. It's like the focus on a projector. If things are out of focus, let's get it back into focus. So we see the real picture.

However 'knowing' alone does not always empower. Therefore, to act according to that knowledge is the sixth power.

6. **Power to Judge:** Gives us the ability and strength to translate an enlightened consciousness into elevated, yet practical action. It's the power to judge accurately who and what you are. You are able to judge, decide, and execute. These are all one single word which the world craves. Every organization and every household *has* the power to execute. Execute, decide, and judge. You are an accurate judge and you do it so that your actions never betray you. You're not fooling yourself in your actions. You haven't deceived yourself. For that, we also spoke about the judges within the framework of *Gulliver's Travels*, and *King Lear*, where they would rather 'plate sin with gold' and break the strong lance of justice. But you are so clear in your judgment that you will never do wrong. For every decision, in every single moment, the two paths will emerge in your vision, and you will have the power to judge which road to take, and you will choose the sure path of truth and fortune.

7. **Power to Face (Courage):** Enables us to direct the light of our truth into the last dark corners of the soul. We find ourselves easily able to face the last of our shortcomings, which, in turn, enables us to handle the difficult situations in our daily life responsibly. As the light grows, the darkness is vanquished. The ability to face with absolute courage the heartbeat of the soul, a conscience so clear you can face anything. You can take the slaps. The power to face and to face everything accurately.

8. **Power to Cooperate:** This power calls on all the other seven powers to enable them to serve at all times—selflessly, generously, and tirelessly. This is actually what spiritual power is all about: the ability to sustain virtue and goodness in all situations and to help others do so, too. It is not about self-transformation alone; it's about the changes that will take place when enough of us start to live from our highest truth, together in unity and harmony.

    How to bring about the synergy of collective cooperation from everyone, because a lot of the time people beat their heads against a brick wall. 'I need cooperation.' But have they even begun to process those eight powers to reach the point of cooperation? A person doesn't cooperate because he doesn't have the accurate judgment or discernment power. He doesn't have flexibility.

All of these eight super powers are what emerge when you polish that jewel that is you, as you journey through life, founding yourself on the truth. What you give out is what comes back to you. The spiritual needs no amount of money. No amount of wealth or striving for wealth can ever satisfy the inner spirit, which will become empty when you escalate wrongly in life. Being true to ourselves brings us back to true happiness. Cooperation is something that is very necessary because every human being is depleted in those qualities.

Cooperation creates a strategic interdependency. Stephen Covey spoke about being born dependent on your mother's breast and then becoming independent in life, and then coming into the realm of interdependency. That is what brings about wisdom. I put what I have on the table and this is what I know. Can you please tell me what you have? That power of collective cooperation, that centre point, becomes wisdom. Wisdom is what drives us to the best of our lives and where we're supposed to go in achievement.

A BBC report commented that Goldman Sachs can, at times, conduct up to 60 interviews on one individual, looking for the master quality of cooperation. Such is the power of cooperation that in all the current rugged terrain and atmosphere of the business world today, one is still able to keep one's head above water, and continue to visualize a way forward with collective synergy.

The eight powers versus maya / illusion: When you have knowledge and power, it becomes easy to oppose an illusionary lifestyle. To use all the powers at the right time to destroy all forms of illusions and obstacles means to be a 'master' authority. One can become a lighthouse and give the experience of the rays of the eight powers through oneself while walking and moving around.

When a precious, flawless diamond is placed in front of a light, you can see many colours in it. Similarly, when you access and polish the diamond within, as you walk and move around, there will be the experience of the rays of the eight powers from you. Some will receive a feeling of the power of tolerance, and others will receive a feeling of the strength in the power of your decision-making.

Some will have a feeling of one power and others will have a feeling of another power.

A practical example is one whose every action is one that inspires everyone.

The embodiment of powers is to always transform excuses and reasons into solutions and constantly move forward.

Only when you wake up do you realize you were sleeping. Try it tomorrow morning. When you wake up in bed you say, 'Oh, I was actually sleeping'. A lot of people are sleepwalking without having this inner journey. In terms of comprehending the roles of the Supreme, there is almost a magic involved in this life.

God is a spiritual architect who can build all of the walls and bridges that will take us through life. He is also a spiritual surgeon that can perform true open-heart surgery painlessly, and without any synthetic anaesthetic. Only once one agrees to open one's heart to the Master Surgeon, the metaphysical surgery is performed clinically and painlessly. The pain is experienced via relief, a release, a liberation.

The entry gate into illusion is driven by vices. The exit gate from illusion is driven by virtues. Stay true and live in the realm of truth, or instead be driven by vices into that realm of falsehood. Then you've become as worthless as a tossed shell. As for sharing, if you can share organizationally or if you can share in families, then you will be driven by the inner wisdom that can really make your life like a shining diamond. When that diamond shines brightly, it's sharing that multiplies your fortune. As we have stated earlier, money is like manure (*a great fertiliser*) and we must spread it around, and it is a potent fertilizer to bring fruition in your life and the lives of many. Money is physical and perishable, but the diamonds of spiritual wisdom are subtle and imperishable. That is very important, how we share, and how we cooperate, and how we grow. Whatever qualities that are depleted in us, we are able to access them through interdependency, through respect, through regard. If a person is ready to share, 'Oh, sure. I can help you out. Yes', is the kind of cooperative response you will have in your life.

The deeper the CEO understands this and opens his third eye, the divine eye of knowledge, the divine intellect, the greater his ability to accept to change and transform for the better. In reciprocation, God cleans up the past karmic debt. It's fine. There are times we work through ignorance. We build up debt. It's been likened to God standing there and saying, 'Well, here. I'm going to sign your check for you now'.

You say, 'No, no. I can handle it myself.' There is a time of spiritual blindness. Let's look at a particular scenario which highlights the theme of blindness. Someone comes and pushes you in the back and you fall flat on your face into a pool of mud. An observer asks, 'What are you going to do now?' You instantly react, 'Well, I'm going to get up and beat this guy up.' The same observer alerts you that the perpetrator is eight feet tall. You think, 'Oh, then I'd rather run away.' But then the same observer informs you that the very person who pushed you is actually a blind man. With this sudden paradigm shift, even with your face all muddy, your gut instinct and immediate response will be, 'I'm sorry. Can I help you?'

Through such spiritual blindness and ignorance, there are many people who do many things. The formula for love is forgiveness. A lot of people say they can forgive but they'll never forget. Or they'll forget but they'll never forgive. The formula is simple. Learn the lesson. Forgive and forget. That is an expression of love. We've come full circle back to love, the original love.

THE FORMULA: 'LEARN, FORGIVE, AND FORGET = EXPRESSION OF LOVE'

If we are not ready to journey through this life and constantly learn from everything, forgive and forget as we move along, then we will never be able to experience true love and be guided by true things. Again, we've come full circle to a 'love-filled relationship being the deepest desire of the human soul'.

ANECDOTE OF THE MONK

TAKE ONE: THE UNENLIGHTENED MONK

A monk is being chased by a ferocious lion and they reach the edge of a cliff, so the monk jumps off the cliff to escape the lion, and luckily grabs onto a branch of a strawberry plant on the way down. Unfortunately the monk notices there are two rats chewing away at the branch of the strawberry plant. The monk nervously looks way down below seeing and feeling the gravity pull of a daunting valley with a rugged terrain inviting him for a sure and painful death. The lion continues growling, and rats continue chewing, and the cowardly monk dies a thousand deaths before his free-fall into the graveyard of the valley of the shadow of death.

TAKE TWO: RECAP: THE ENLIGHTENED MONK – A SAGE FOR OUR TIMES

The monk is being chased by a ferocious lion, a symbol of the past. There is a rearview mirror warning which states that 'objects in the mirror are closer than they appear'. Imagination is also like a ferocious lion. The monk jumps off the cliff to escape the lion, grabs onto a branch of a strawberry plant on the side of the cliff, the symbol of sweetness and beauty and the present moment. Way down below is the valley, the symbol of death. This is the 'valley of the shadow of death' that we all traverse through in this day and age where there are no guarantees for our next minute.

There are two rats chewing away at the branch of the strawberry plant. That's a symbol of time eating away at our pleasurable life. *La dolce vita* refers to the sweetness of life that Italians talk about in terms of squeezing pleasure out from a hard working day. However, the monk is purely focused on the beauty and the sweetness of the colourful strawberry plant. He stays focused because it doesn't matter about the past. It doesn't matter about time or the rats scurrying and eating away at the plant. It doesn't matter what's below.

He remains so focused on the sweetness of the colourful straw-berry plant and the moment, that the deeper he goes into that sweetness, the more he becomes enlightened about the imperish-able moment of time. In becoming a knower of the three aspects of time, his yesterday, this moment, and tomorrow, he is able to dispel the rats. The rats were an illusion, like time is an illusion of *maya*, eating away at your day.

When the monk becomes enlightened, his being emanates a blinding pure light which dispels the rats. Like flipping a switch on in a darkened room, so the rats scurry away. He is able to dispel that illusion of time eating away at the plant. He focuses deeply on the strawberry plant, which symbolizes the power of now, the sweetness of the moment. Staying close to physical death allows one to remain sweet.

Dying alive (killing the vices, and living within the privilege of virtues) in the moment allows one to dive deep into God's ocean of knowledge and fathom all the depths to access all the treasures of the deep. Purity, transparency, clarity is remaining 100 per cent in the current moment and being totally focused and giving of yourself.

> *'You give but little when you give of your possessions. It is when you give of yourself that you truly give.'*
>
> —KHALIL GIBRAN

Accuracy is like a brilliantly cut diamond. Accuracy comes from knowing how to make the point between mind and matter a harmonious one. When you are able to give 100 per cent to each moment in your life and each person in your life, in your interactions and not shortchanging them with a scattered mind, the Om is on. Om is 'I am'. My original being is Om. Our target is *Om Shanti*, I am a peaceful soul. Sinning is missing the target of *Om Shanti* and becoming peaceless. In your innings in life, avoid sinning or missing the target. The innings can be referring to a cricket match, baseball game or any innings in sports. But avoid sinning.

Focusing the mind on the supreme. We receive the eight powers, the eight powers we discussed. The colours of the rainbow which merge into one and become a laser beam of pure white light, in order to become an embodiment of a great leader who is *constantly* seated on the swing of truth and happiness, with knowledge as one of the ropes, and union (yoga) with the Supreme as the other. In the words of Ray Bradbury, 'You've got to jump off cliffs all the time, and build your wings on the way down'. This is definitely possible if one of your wings is knowledge and the other is union (yoga) with God.

Where there is truth the soul dances. The boat of truth may rock but it will never sink. When the light of the eight powers stays with you, illusion can never come close to you. You rock in constant happiness. The rats scurry away, saving the monk from that *achanak* or sudden nature of physical death in this age.

Even in *Kaliyug* (the age of darkness), time becomes a friend. The ferocious lion smiles, and becomes a guard against illusion. It reminds us of our happy past while we are able to concentrate on the sweetness of the moment. The valley below becomes filled with the flood of knowledge. Knowledge is the font of wisdom, and "Sapientia Fons Vitae"—Wisdom is the Fountain of Life.

As the monk focuses deeper into the moment, the lion becomes a courageous friend and protector. The third eye of knowledge is open and he is a knower of the three aspects of time. He then becomes a spinner of the discus of self-realization and he is able to win everything in life. With determined faith in his intellect, he is completely carefree, knowing that both his destiny and his victory are guaranteed. The victory is guaranteed.

The three I's are sitting and vying for power. He lets go of the I of arrogance. He lets go of the I of disheartenment. He submerges it. The eye of soul consciousness emerges. The two I's of arrogance and disheartenment lose their power and soul consciousness takes over. He experiences profound peace, contentment and bliss. The valley below becomes a boundless ocean.

The beauty and attraction allows us to let go of the strawberry branch and say a timely, not sudden, 'au revoir' to the lion and go into a free fall, detach and leap into the cool ocean, where we achieve our super-sensuous joy and drown ourselves to die alive. To exist in a life fully focused on our eternity, our imperishable self. To go to the bottom of the ocean of pure thoughts and become an embodiment of silence.

Let your past experiences become a bestower of fortune and let the blessings emerge. Remain busy in this service of sharing the best of yourself with the world. Thus, the monk becomes a sage and the Lord of Light smiles.

The monk delves into the ocean where he's completely safe. The deeper he swims, the closer he gets to those gems we found at the beginning of the book, the ones we share with those we love.

We're ending where we began, with the cycle of life. And so, we come full circle, in the great cycle of life.

The more you absorb and blend the knowledge of truth and you look through the viewfinder of your divine eye, as a detached observer you look at your life as a movie. You edit out the negativity. 'Take One, Take Two, Take Three'—edit out all the mistakes, the Miss-Takes, go accurately through the rushes, and present your most inspired 'director's cut' for the world to see how truly brilliant you are.

When we realise and truly experience we are on a journey through time itself, we will become masters of time.

> *'What we call the beginning is often the end. And to make an end is to make a beginning. The end is where we start from.'*
>
> —T.S. ELIOT

I will never be the same...again...

All unreferenced quotations titled "Gems from the depth of the Ocean" - BK World Spiritual University

BOOKS / INFORMATION LEAFLETS

18 Chapters of the Gita—B.K.I.S. (B.K. Information Service)

Stress Management—B.K.I.S.

Inner Leadership—B.K.I.S.

The Alpha Point—A Glimpse of God—Anthony Strano

Experience Massive Amounts of Energy—All Day, Every Day—Anthony Robbins

Awaken the Giant Within—Anthony Robbins

PowerTalk—Anthony Robbins interview with Dr. Wayne Dyer

You Can Heal Yourself—Louise Hay

Love Signs—Linda Goodman

The Seven Habits of Highly Effective People—Steven Covey

"The 8th Habit" from *Effectiveness to Greatness (To Live, Learn, Love & Leave a Legacy)*—Steven Covey

The One Minute Manager—Kenneth Blanchard & Spencer Johnson

Autobiography of a Yogi—Parmahansa Yogananda

Spiritual Greatness—Insights for Expressing Personal Excellence in Challenging Times—Dadi Janki

The Prophet—Khalil Gibran

God's Wisdom—Sister Jayanti

The Little Soul and the Sun—Neale Donald Walsh

Love—Jewels from the words of Abdul-Baha

The Trial—Franz Kafza

The Franklin's Tale—Geoffrey Chaucer (The Canterbury Tales)

Who's Afraid of Virginia Woolf?—Edward Albee

Waiting for Godot—Samuel Beckett

The Party—Harold Pinter

Intimate Behaviour—Desmond Morris

AUDIO-VISUAL / PERSONAL LECTURES/ MAGAZINE ARTICLES:

"Putting the One Minute Manager to Work"—The A.C.H.I.E.V.E. (MENT) Model – K. Blanchard & S.Johnson

"Surrender / Submission"—Dadi Janki – Golbal Director of BK World Spiritual University

"Churning Power - Being Lost in Love"—Dadi Janki

"Transformation Depends on Me"—Dadi Janki

"Inner Leadership – Managing from Within"—B.K.I.S.

"The Psychic and the Yogi"—a close encounter forum

between Uri Gellar &Dadi Janki @ the Albert Hall

"Accurate Link with God"—Anthony Strano

"The Story of My Experiments with Truth"—Mahatma Gandhi

"Meditation"—Foundation course in RAJ YOGA meditation

"Apocalypse Now"—Newsweek Magazine

"The American army's secret weapon" (Prozac)—Newsweek Magazine

"Win at Work"—A Reader's Digest guide

Mountain streams—Christian reflection

"Inside Pfizer's palace coup" Peter Elkind & Jennifer Reinhold
with Doris Burke: Fortune Magazine –Aug 2011

"Atlantis – Past and To Come"

Printed in the USA
CPSIA information can be obtained
at www.ICGtesting.com
JSHW012050140824
68134JS00035B/3356